SOME HELP ALONG THE WAY

A Journey
of Faith

Terence Michael O'Gara

2025 Second Printing

Some Help Along the Way: A Journey of Faith

ISBN 979-8-218-94057-7

Copyright © 2024 by Terence Michael O'Gara

All rights reserved. No portion of this book may be reproduced, stored in an electronic retrieval system, or transmitted in any form or by any means—electronic, mechanical, photocopy, recording, or any other—except for brief quotations in printed reviews, without the prior permission of the author.

Printed in the United States of America

"Out of the crooked timber of humanity,
no straight line was ever made."
—Immanuel Kant

Contents

Introduction	7
Prologue	15
Chapter 1 Making the Grade School	17
Chapter 2 High School, the Wonder Years	21
Chapter 3 A College Boy Now	29
Chapter 4 The Chosen	37
Chapter 5 The Challenged	47
Chapter 6 "Did he say Grand Forks?"	71
Chapter 7 Joel Schrimsher	75
Chapter 8 Crewed Up and Screwed Up	81
Chapter 9 Reckless Abandonment	95
Chapter 10 "Play Ball!"	101
Chapter 11 Sheppard Air Force Base	107
Chapter 12 From Right Seat to Left Seat	125
Chapter 13 A Changing of Uniforms	133
Chapter 14 Faith Reborn	135
Epilogue	143
Afterword	147
Acknowledgments	153

Introduction

Hello, my full name is Terence Michael O'Gara. I go by Terry. I was born in the mid-1950's, and most who grew up in that decade would agree a lot has changed between now and then. I was the second of four children raised by two wonderful parents as an Irish Catholic in the Midwest. We went to Mass every Sunday, said grace before dinner, had fish on Fridays (pre-Vatican II), served as altar boys (my younger sister was ineligible for such duties), and spent twelve years in the Catholic school system. My mother's maiden name was O'Connell, so in many ways we were as typical an Irish Catholic family as you might ever find.

I graduated from high school in the spring of 1973, and by the fall, I was attending a state university. By the time my freshman year ended, I had stopped attending Mass and lost my belief in a Supreme Being. My parents were very hurt by this, but I felt like I was just moving on from a quaint idea from my earlier life. It was time to grow up and deal with the real world. I graduated from college, found a profession, and a few years later met a woman. We decided to marry, and out of respect for my parents, we married in the Church. The year was 1985.

Life began to move faster. We had two children who were growing up quickly. My wife and I found ourselves juggling the demands of family life with our professional lives, and at times it was difficult. I sometimes caught myself wondering how my parents managed to raise the four of us and make it look easy. I guess it inspired me to follow in their footsteps, going back to my faith (albeit slowly), attending Mass on Sundays, saying grace before dinner, taking pride in seeing our children as altar servers, and educating them for twelve years in the Catholic school system. Friday-night fish fries were replaced with Sunday-morning pancake breakfasts in the school cafeteria, but otherwise it didn't seem like a lot changed from one generation to the next. The technology had improved. The station wagon was replaced by the minivan and as personal preferences go, I liked the pancakes better than the fish. But I now had a real respect and appreciation for my parents and the choices they made for us in childhood.

Our children grew up and left home. I retired at age sixty after having a good career in a tough profession, and I looked forward to a quiet life. For the first few years I got what I hoped for. I established a routine that suited me. We were financially secure, and the kids were self-sufficient.

Then the pandemic hit. A "two-week lockdown to flatten the curve" turned into a seemingly endless, hopeless ordeal. The number of new infections and deaths from the disease was the top story in the daily news broadcasts. Suddenly, the country was scrambling to provide oxygen ventilators for everyone on death's doorstep from the infection, and there just weren't enough to go around. Rationing was instituted for these critical medical devices, and a solution was offered. A WWII–era manufacturing law was dusted off, and in the blink of an eye, the Ford Motor Company, among others, was conscripted to build ventilators in plants where cars were formerly produced. And no manufacturer's warranties were offered on them. The locked-down residents of New York City, one of the hardest hit areas in the country, took to opening their apartment windows at seven o'clock every evening to beat on pots and pans in appreciation of health care professionals and their round-the-clock fight to care for the sick. It was a wonderful, yet heartrending gesture in the face of the deadly, chaotic environment we found ourselves in. The cacophony those pots and pans made was also a plea for normalcy and real human contact heard around the globe.

In the midst of all this, I had my own personal concerns. My wife and I had reached the age where we were considered to be highly susceptible to the infection. We were both healthy and fit. We had spent a lifetime exercising and maintaining healthy habits. Still, stories of twenty- and thirty-somethings who lost their battles with COVID-19 regularly filled the news outlets. And my children unfortunately followed in my footsteps, jettisoning their faith early in their adult years.

I got to experience with my children how my parents must have felt when I left the Church during my college years. Yet they held out hope for me, prayed for me, and with time I made my way back. With my children and COVID-19, it felt different. When I was growing up, roughly 70 percent of the country's population claimed to have religious faith and regularly practiced it. Since the 1960s, however, that percentage has been gradually falling to the point where less than half the population can make the same claim now. Religious belief seemed to be slowly dying, especially among the young, and having the church doors shut for months by the authorities didn't help matters. What was going to happen once they were allowed to reopen? Would everyone come back, grateful for the opportunity to worship once again, or would the pews be sparsely filled and the decline in belief accelerate even more? It was an open question, but I might not be around to see the answer if I contracted the disease. And I needed to do something besides praying for my children if I were to let them know how important God was in my life.

So, the pandemic lockdown and my children's lack of faith in an increasingly faithless world forced my hand. I picked up a pen and began to write about my life and God's influence in it so I could leave it behind for them once I left this world. It took a while, but we were in lockdown, so I plodded on, hoping not to contract the infection before I finished. My son, who is tech-savvy, built our computer for us and in his estimation thought we would never need a word-processing program. So, I ended up old school, going through reams of paper and gallons of ink before I was through. I finally finished on Christmas Eve of 2020.

It occurred to me a few days after I finished that I could use an editor. After all, I am not a writer, and I knew I needed my best effort if I was going to change their minds about God and His Church. An editor could point out spots where the story could use some polishing. After investigating alternatives, I ended up choosing my older brother, a retired journalist and editor. He promised not to mention a word about my lockdown project, and I got a family discount with his efforts.

So, the story was polished to our satisfaction, and I stuck two copies of it in our safe deposit box at the bank. It would be there waiting for the children along with the will and other papers once I passed away. The kids could then learn about their father, his life, and how he rediscovered his faith after losing it. Considering both of them and all the circumstances I wrote about, I felt it would benefit them the most once I was gone.

I felt a wonderful sense of satisfaction after having completed this project. For one, I was able to finish it, surviving both the pandemic and writing cramps in my right hand. It was now safely locked away, hopefully not to be seen for many years to come. I had never planned on sharing any of what I wrote about. But if it made a difference in my children's lives, the effort was worth it. By the time it saw the light of day, they might be more inclined to accept what I wrote. Not that there was anything nefarious spread across the pages they would be reading. My hope was by then they might be dealing with children of their own and have accumulated more of life's richness and wisdom from their experiences. Perhaps this would make them more open and accepting of its message.

So, I left the bank with almost a sense of elation. All the hours of recollection, pondering, organizing, writing and rewriting, frustration and late, late nights were behind me. I could get back to a more normal routine since restrictions were starting to ease. Thank goodness, we were emerging from a long, dark night.

Yet the wonderful sense of satisfaction I felt coming out of the bank was short-lived. I soon found myself waking up in the middle of the night and unable to get back to sleep for hours at a time. I felt something was missing from my story. Yet, how could it be possible? I covered everything and then some. Still, I couldn't shake the feeling. So, I went back and added what might be one of the longest acknowledgment sections ever written to expand on characters and events. When it was through, I was pleased with the results and hoped this would quell the anxiety and restless nights. I could really have used some sleep.

Unfortunately, it didn't work, and I was still up half the night. It turns out the nocturnal restlessness had to do with another issue involving my plan. After spending a lot of time alone in the church praying for guidance, I decided to change course. With great reluctance and a lot of hesitation, I concluded I needed to share my story more broadly. It's certainly not something I wanted to do. It really goes against my nature. But I have been given a lot of undeserved help throughout my life. I accepted the help while doing my best not to acknowledge it, and now the bill has come due. And it's not possible to pay on the installment plan, either. Full payment is required.

At this point it would be fair to ask what caused me to change my mind, breaking a promise to myself about discussing my life and how I came back to the Church, and then putting it out there for everyone to see. Honestly, I hope the effort I made helps others, especially my children, to come back to their faith. Life makes little sense without it. But there is also an element of fear in my motivation. In Matthew's gospel, Jesus tells the story about the master and his three servants. This master gave each

Introduction

servant talents according to their abilities and then went away on a journey. When he returned, he wanted an account of what they had done with what they had been given. I don't want to be like the servant in the story who buried his talent.

I also should address an issue brought to my attention by my wonderful wife of thirty-eight years. It has to do with primacy of place and how this story was written. As I stated earlier, I originally planned for this work to be read by my two children after my passing. I painstakingly wrote it by hand and put two copies for them in the safe deposit box at our nearby bank. That plan didn't quite work out for me, so what you have before you now is the result of my effort to share this story. Yet, I did the best I could to retain all the care and concern, love, and intimacy of its original scope—that is, as a father leaving a work for his two children. Throughout the narrative you will find me addressing them directly, ignoring the wider audience I included "with great reluctance and a lot of hesitation." I just ask that you indulge me in those many instances and consider yourselves fellow travelers with them as the story unfolds.

So let me end the introduction here by saying this book isn't for everyone. If you are hesitant about starting, let me encourage you to read the prologue and to the point where I am ending my freshman year in high school. It shouldn't take more than ten minutes, tops. If, at this point, you feel the narrative lacks credibility, I recommend you put the story down and go do something else. Life is too short to waste your time and reading this would be a waste of your time. However, if you find yourself intrigued, I urge you to buckle up and continue. It's going to be a bumpy ride.

Prologue

I started this project in the spring of 2020. A lot was going on at the time. Always looking for a way to challenge myself, I took up CrossFit training well past my sixtieth birthday. It didn't end well for me. I managed to injure my shoulder enough to require surgery. My arm was in a sling for a month, and the recovery was very slow and painful. Your mother and I also forgot for a moment that our lives were full enough and purchased an eleven-week-old puppy we named Shadow. Her arrival was certainly a big adjustment in our lives—perhaps too big. Nonetheless, she quickly became a valued member of the family.

The biggest surprise of that spring was the COVID-19 virus. It raced across the globe, causing the world's governments to impose lockdowns on their citizens and whole economies to close up shop. I took advantage of the lockdown to write about some occurrences in my life that I never shared with anyone—at all. It began modestly, but as the lockdown grew in length, so did the size and scope of my efforts. Long-forgotten memories resurfaced to pour out from my pen and add to my story as the lockdown dragged on. The writing sometimes proved to be difficult and sometimes quite exhilarating. But good days or bad, I stuck with it, and when the effort was finally complete, it turned out far better than anything I could have hoped or planned for. What made the effort so rewarding though, was my intention all along to share it with both of you. What I wrote about borders on the fantastic: certainly, more than just an oddity or mere coincidence. I hope it will help bring you back to your religious faith and its practices as it did for me. And as a small aside, I hope it provides more of my personal history for you both, something I never really could learn about my father and his years of early struggle that shaped him in adulthood.

CHAPTER 1
Making the Grade School

I was born in December of 1954 at Saint Joseph's Hospital in Flint, Michigan. My parents moved there right after they were married in June of 1950 because my father had a job offer to work in a radio station as a sales executive. My brother Hugh ("Clancy") soon came along in May of 1951. I was following him about three-and-a-half years later because of a series of earlier miscarriages experienced by my mother. This time, though, things were very different for her. After those pregnancies tragically ended before full-term, I was very willing to stay the full term and then some. When I finally arrived, I was two weeks or more overdue. None of the staff had ever seen an infant so large. I set a hospital record for length and weight. According to Mom, the nurses were "very sympathetic" of her struggle to carry me whenever they brought me into nurse. As I grew older, there would be similar instances of sympathy offered to her about me; these instances, however, always involved my behavior.

As a child I was high-energy, high-maintenance. When it came time for me to start school it was no surprise to Mom that this kind of behavior would carry over into the classroom. She was right, of course. Mothers usually are when it comes to their children. Although I have no memory of it, she said I was sent to the principal's office on my first day of kindergarten. I was there waiting for her when she came to pick me up after school. Not a good beginning for my introduction to formal education, nor did it get better for me there as the year wore on. At the end of the term, my kindergarten teacher, Mrs. Reimus, told Mom she expected me to end up a "juvenile delinquent."

Still, that was the public school system. I hadn't been introduced to the "A-Team" yet, which consisted of the nuns of St. John's parochial school in Davison, Michigan. Looking back on it, I have nothing but sympathy and admiration for those fine women of God. They had as many as fifty children per classroom. That their students could achieve any significant learning in such a challenging environment is a testimony to their dedication and skill.

Not surprisingly, their students' remarkable academic achievements were earned using healthy doses of discipline. Self-discipline in the classroom, however, was not my strong suit. Again, I learned from my mother sometime after I completed the fifth grade that my teacher, Sister Herman (that's correct—Sister Herman), had lowered all my grades one level to all Bs because I kept turning around in line and talking. I told Mom that Sister Herman, in a frank talk we had during a recess period, had asked if I liked her. She was visibly upset over something I had said and felt exasperated and angry. I was equally exasperated and angry with her, so I bluntly replied, no,

I didn't. My mother, always a saint, patiently explained what a difficult job Sister Herman had with all those students assigned to her and my behavior in line and my rudeness during our conversation didn't help matters. Secretly though, I don't think Mom liked Sister Herman much after that either.

After I completed fifth grade the family left Michigan for Omaha, Nebraska. So, with a new school, new classmates, and new nuns, my behavior in the class improved. It certainly wasn't perfect. I still felt the occasional slap on the face delivered by a nun for a comment better left unspoken. But at least my grades weren't being lowered for turning around in line and talking.

CHAPTER 2
High School, the Wonder Years

I left Saint James Elementary to attend Archbishop Rummel High School in the fall of 1969. It was an all-boys Catholic high school populated mostly with Catholic kids I had seen and competed against in grade-school sports. Among these former competitors, I soon found friends that I still have and cherish. Tragically though, death took one shortly before he was to make the valedictorian address at our graduation and took another one a year later. Both were due to avoidable accidents.

But I am getting ahead of myself here. I need to bring the timeline back to the end of my freshman year, the spring of 1970. By this time, I was all of fifteen years old, sitting alone in an otherwise empty classroom during a free period and trying to decide what I was going to do with my life. That was a pretty daunting task, especially for a fifteen-year-old, but even then, I had a penchant for planning for the future—which seemed so distant back then.

As I sat there, alone with my thoughts, trying to decide what I should do, I realized how many plausible choices there were, and I needed a way to narrow them down. So, I started by deciding which things I really didn't want to do, to eliminate those choices right from the start. As you might expect, that list was easier to assemble. It also helped define items, or should I say requirements, that determined what kind of career I was interested in. I knew I wouldn't be happy sitting behind a desk in an office five days a week. Nor was I looking for some dull field like accounting. I wanted something that was exciting and adventurous, where travel was involved, and you made a lot of money. A quiet thought crept into my mind, proffering a solution. "Be an airline pilot" was heard and initially met with an enthusiastic response on my part. Still an adolescent and already I possessed a fear of being trapped in life as a nine-to-five careerist. Certainly, there are no office desks in a cockpit, so, yes, "Wonderful choice!" I thought, "But how do you become an airline pilot?" The only experience I had with airplanes was a round trip to Los Angeles on United Airlines to visit Disneyland about five years earlier. "What am I supposed to do to fly for an airline?"

"You join the Air Force," came the obvious reply.

"Okay," I thought, a bit forlornly, "so, I guess I'm joining the Air Force."

Despite my initial enthusiasm, this whole exercise of future planning had the effect of leaving me unsettled. For one, the process took about ten minutes, which for me was very uncharacteristic. For such an important decision as this, I would normally go to the library to check out material about flying and the airline profession. After perusing the material, I would make a list of advantages and disadvantages. Then I would deliberate, carefully choosing whether to go forward with pursuing it. If I decided that, indeed, it was worth pursuing, I would assemble another list, this time detailing potential risks so I could figure out a way to minimize them to ensure success.

This reads as if I should have gone into securities analysis rather than flying. But this deviation from normal, personal behavior wasn't the most unsettling aspect of this exercise in career planning. The most unsettling aspect was even though I was alone in the room, the quiet thought that crept into my mind wasn't the product of my own prefrontal cortex. It came from somewhere, but it definitely didn't come from me.

Let that sink in for a while. Then again, you always suspected your father was a little bit crazy. Now there is evidence dating all the way back to when he was fifteen years old.

Of course, I was startled by all this, and I certainly wasn't going to tell anyone about the details of how I decided on a career path. When my friends and I started talking about what we wanted to do for a living, I could offer an answer, just not the circumstances that led me to it.

Yet, what a life-changing ten minutes that was. Before going into that empty room during a study hall my freshman year, the idea of joining the Air Force was about the last thing my friends or I would have suspected of me. The only thing less likely was joining a seminary.

So now that I knew what I wanted to do, I needed a plan, and the first step was to find out what it took to fly for the Air Force. This posed a problem because this was at the height of the Vietnam War, and my mother was like most mothers whose son expressed interest in the military during wartime. She had a two-word response when she found out—"Absolutely not!"—thus providing me with my first of many hurdles to overcome on my way to the airlines. It took patience and persistence on my part to bring both Mom and Dad around, but they grudgingly accepted my reasoning in the end. A big part of their acceptance, I sensed, was their thinking there was no way in hell their skinny, fifteen-year-old son with the smart mouth was cut out for the military, let alone a pilot. They sent me off to Offutt Air Force Base with their blessing to talk with specialists and take exams to see if I was physically and mentally qualified. When the results of the exams came back, I am sure they were a little disappointed to learn I was.

Academics in high school proved easy enough. With plenty of study halls built into the schedule, I never really had homework. My grades were fine, and I enjoyed playing sports on some of the school teams and with my friends. I was still committed to my future career plans, so I was always working or hustling for money because one thing I discovered early was learning to fly was expensive. And I wanted a head start before I joined the Air Force. So, I had a paper route, caddied at the Omaha Country Club, was a ranch hand for a summer, and worked at JC Penney as a maintenance man trying to save enough for lessons. I finally earned enough to start taking lessons just before graduation. But I am getting ahead of myself again.

My junior year of high school brought questions to my mind

about where I wanted to attend college. Like my freshman year, I was confronted with an important decision to make with too many options to sort through, and I needed to narrow the field. So, just as I had done as a freshman, I began my search for post-secondary education with what I didn't want. Number one was I didn't want to go to Nebraska. Among all my classmates who were actually going to college, Nebraska was their overwhelming choice and honestly, I wasn't too impressed with many of them. Nor did I want to attend the Air Force Academy. I was going to graduate from an all-male high school. I didn't want to graduate from an all-male military academy too. In the counselor's office at school there was a big, thick volume containing reviews of all major and minor colleges and universities in the country, so I opened it up and began a haphazard search during a study hall. As I was paging through, I saw Colorado State University listed and was surprised that Colorado had another major university in their state system besides the University of Colorado, a fierce football rival to Nebraska. As I read on, I became intrigued because they offered an atmospheric science degree, one of only two places in the world with such a program (the other required that you matriculate in Moscow). I also noted the university had an Air Force Reserve Officer Training Corps (AFROTC) program that I needed for commissioning along with my degree to get into flight training. As I was mulling all of this over in my mind, I experienced the same kind of mental direction I was given as a freshman. I "heard" this was where I needed to go for college.

Once again, I was startled by this. Twice now in fewer than two years this had happened to me. I had tried to forget about the first time it happened because as time passed, I frankly didn't want to acknowledge that quiet voice. It was delusional, really, to believe it actually occurred. It was far more plausible to believe that I came up with the plan on my own without any outside guidance or direction. I was just somehow fooling myself as a freshman. No strange voices in my head, no sir! And now it was back a second time!

I calmed myself down with some effort and thought about the advice I was given to attend CSU. It made sense from a career standpoint. Getting a degree in atmospheric science along with an Air Force flying background would certainly look good on a resume for any major airline. So, I sent out applications to a few state universities in the Midwest, but during spring break, CSU was the only school Dad and I visited. While we were there, we stopped by the AFROTC recruiting booth and spent some time learning about course sign up, commitment, degree requirements, and Undergraduate Pilot Training (UPT). It was a valuable stop just for the effect it had on changing my father's perspective about joining the military. The drive back turned out to be pleasant, even if the scenery was dull.

My senior year flew by. I gave up playing basketball for the school team to earn money for college and flying lessons, not that my absence on the roster was any big loss for the team. I was finally challenged in my studies enough to have homework by enrolling in chemistry. Unfortunately, I did it the last semester of the school term, so to earn a full year credit, I crammed two semesters into one. Had I been smarter, I would have signed up for it in the fall term. I don't know what I was thinking at the time.

The most notable event for my senior year of high school was the loss of a good friend in a work-related accident at his part-time job. I was talking with him and another good friend, just the three of us in a classroom before he left for work. The next day in homeroom before classes began, I learned of his passing. That other friend drowned in a lake the following year. That should have been a wake-up call for my faith, but of course, it wasn't. I couldn't process their loss very well. I was eighteen years old, going on nineteen at the time, so I did my best not to think about it, and that I did very well. I used my career plans and the drive to achieve them like a medicinal balm to cover over my grief at their demise. Perspective would have to wait.

CHAPTER 3
A College Boy Now

The summer between high school and college stretched out before me now, and it seemed almost interminable. Thanks to my older brother Clancy, I was soon filling the time between high school and college working at the Safeway bakery near the Union Pacific train yard downtown. He worked there the previous summer, and they liked him so much they called to ask him back. He declined because he was a college graduate now and was looking for a white-collar job. So, they asked "if there were any more like him at home." And thus began my summertime career as a baker. It was hard, physical labor, usually in the middle of the night, manning a spot on the production line and always at a temperature of at least 100 degrees Fahrenheit. The first few weeks almost killed me, but I couldn't die because the money was too good to pass up. So, I survived, saved the money, and left for school motivated to study hard. Otherwise, I knew where I could end up in life.

Some Help Along the Way

So it was now after Labor Day, 1973. Summer was over, and school was about to start for me. Clancy, who had graduated from the University of Missouri four months earlier with a journalism degree, was driving me out to Fort Collins, Colorado, just east of the Rockies. We got up early that morning, loaded up the family's Plymouth Duster with my few belongings, and headed west as fast as we dared in that car. Fortunately, it held together.

We arrived at CSU in the evening and found my dorm room. Clancy spent the night there with me and left early the next morning. I registered for classes in the big school gym across the street from my dorm and was now officially a college student. In my mind, the only difficulty I might have would be finding where all my classrooms were located on campus. I was about to find out what the word "hubris" meant.

It turned out that college courses were more difficult than I thought they would be, and I soon came to recognize I was academically unprepared for them. For many of my fellow classmates, this was not the case. So, the first whole year was spent playing catch up, trying to learn how to take lecture notes, studying, preparing for exams, writing papers, and all the while trying not to get discouraged. Some days were better than others.

Also, at this time I stopped attending Mass on Sunday. I was a college student now and felt that twelve years of Catholic education was enough for me. I didn't need to carry that habit of Sunday Mass with me to Fort Collins. Clancy had stopped attending after he started college, so there was family precedence. Also, that twelve years of Catholic education wasn't paying off too well here at CSU where I was struggling just to pass all my courses. Being Catholic was actually working against my goals because of the education I received. So, I soon forgot about my Sunday obligation and never even located a Catholic Church during my time in Fort Collins.

I headed back to Omaha after the school year ended with a hard-earned C+ average and found out the bakery had been waking my parents up repeatedly over the course of several nights asking if I was back yet. They were quite anxious for my return from school. Despite my meager academic success at CSU, I was determined to go back, so when the bakery called that night, I got up, put on my "baker's whites" and drove downtown to 11th and Davenport to clock in. As usual, by the time I clocked out sometime during the morning or even the afternoon, I would be covered in a mixture of sweat, oil, and flour that would not come off easily in the shower. I hadn't even been home for eight hours, and I was already back to my summer routine—a routine that was going to repeat itself over the next four years, even after I graduated from CSU and was waiting to go to Undergraduate Pilot Training.

Yet even though it was physically demanding work on a production line, usually in the middle of the night, I was grateful to be back. Dad had left the sales manager's job at KETV and started his own one-man advertising firm. This meant money was tight for the family as he had to assemble a client list from scratch. My being on that production line meant he didn't have to shoulder all the burden of family expenses and my college tuition too. One could say the bakery experience and the circumstances leading up to it were a blessing in disguise.

I had come home after my first year of college disappointed with the overall results of my efforts. I learned early that I was not prepared for high-level math and could not learn it on the fly, so I switched majors to psychology and still my grades were pedestrian. The one bright spot was that I passed my pilot's flight exam during the winter break so I could rent an airplane when I had some free time and favorable weather.

But it didn't sit well with me that all the effort I put into my classes was not being reflected in my test scores and grades. I had to figure out a way to do better with my sophomore year approaching. I came up with a few ideas while working and looked forward to implementing them when I returned to Fort Collins, but I felt chastened, recalling my first few days on campus. College success, indeed, proved much more difficult than simply finding all the classrooms for my courses scattered across the campus. I figured that cocky attitude of mine should have earned my picture in the dictionary for the definition of the word "hubris."

Summer ended, and I headed back to Fort Collins, this time driving a high-mileage 1969 Ford F-100 pickup I purchased with my bakery earnings. It was the fall of 1974, and the Vietnam War was winding down to the point the Nixon administration had concluded the highly unpopular national draft was no longer necessary. The military would become an all-volunteer service. This had a dramatic effect on the AFROTC program on campus. My freshman class numbered around 125 cadets, which pushed the small military science building to almost burst at the seams with the number of students and staff it held. Returning to class on that first day of my sophomore year, we had shrunk to no more than twenty-five. All good candidates—nonetheless, it was a pretty dramatic change.

The rest of the campus, however, had not changed. It was still a beautiful, spacious university situated in a small Colorado town tucked up against the eastern foothills of the Rockies. By this time, I was a typical college student who could expertly navigate my way between buildings and classrooms during class changeover periods. I wasn't like a floundering fish that came to mind a year earlier when I was first trying to make my way around campus before the next class began.

One day, about a month after sophomore year began, I was making my way across the large, open intramural field that formed most of the western edge of the university. It was a beautiful, warm, sunny day in October, and I was headed for the first of my afternoon classes when I received another quiet message. It said, "If you don't get your grades up, you will lose your pilot training slot." It was delivered like the previous ones—in me but not from me, and equally as surprising. It was also a very chilling prediction on such a warm, beautiful day. I continued to walk towards class as I tried to digest this latest piece of career advice, this time warning me of a hazard on my academic horizon. My first thought was, "Am I crazy? This is the third time this has happened!" At first blush, any sane person would say, "Yes, you need professional help." Of course, seeking professional help would kill any hope of seeing this little adventure through to successful completion, so my choices were limited. I could ignore it, pretend it didn't happen, and see where things went. Or I could act on it and do something about my grades.

Fortunately, that intramural field was long. It gave me time to review how this all started. Because of a ten-minute exercise alone in a classroom my freshman year of high school, I was on a career path that qualified me for an Air Force UPT slot and had me on the road to getting my officer's commission at CSU. If I were being honest with myself, after last year's report card, I needed all the help I could get if I was serious about my career choice. So, if it took voices out of the blue for motivation, I would accept it. By the time I had reached my classroom, I was still a bit surprised by my third voice experience, but I had a new resolve in my academic pursuits. Some changes I had made in my study habits—plus having a year's experience in college to draw on—were already paying dividends for me. But from then on, every quiz, every test, and every paper I treated like it was the deciding factor for attending UPT. You might think this reaction of mine was a bit overwrought, but as it turned out, it may very well have saved my career.

Still, I don't want to pull the curtain back too soon on this drama without providing some background. So, I need to explain that I was studying three to four hours a day, every day, except on weekends when it was a lot more. I was reviewing class notes, reading the textbooks, researching, and writing my papers and actually enjoying the process. It was quite a reversal from my high school years where I hardly ever really studied and was fairly indifferent to the whole educational experience. Yet I still did well back then. But now I was playing for keeps, and results were critical for me. The good news was all that effort paid off in academic success. My grades climbed, and I made the dean's list. This came just in time to face a different challenge and new threat to my career plans. Life sure was moving fast for me in Fort Collins.

My sophomore year ended, and I drove home to Omaha more satisfied and confident I was on track to carry out my plan. My parents relayed to me that the bakery had been clamoring for my return, and sure enough, I was awakened that night by Dad telling me they wanted me as soon as possible. That same scene would play out over the next three years, with me unloading the truck, having dinner and a couple of hours of sleep, then back to work. I never had to call them to let them know I was in town. They called me, even during holiday breaks.

This summer, though, would be different from the others because I was attending AFROTC summer camp. For most of us, this was our first real introduction to military life. There were marching and drilling exercises, saluting, firing ranges, inspections, briefings, athletic competitions, evaluations, and a whole lot more to prepare us for commissioning and to become qualified, capable Air Force officers. It took place in Columbus, Ohio, at Rickenbacker Air Force Base in the month of July and a particularly hot one as Julys go.

My attitude while I was there was not the best. I wasn't planning on being a career Air Force officer like many who attended. So, I just kept my head down and tried not to volunteer when those "opportunities to excel" were offered. I think our training officer figured this out since I was the very last candidate in the squadron who mastered the skill of making up a barrack's bed so tightly a quarter tossed on the blanket would bounce. I was restricted to base for two successive weekends for not passing that milestone in barracks housekeeping.

The biggest highlight of the camp session by far was loading up the cadet squadron into a KC-135 one morning and flying down to an Air Force UPT base in Mississippi for a flight in a T-37. The T-37 was the initial jet trainer for pilot training, and pound-for-pound, the loudest jet in the Air Force inventory. It was fully aerobatic, which the instructor pilot couldn't demonstrate because the weather was too cloudy. Nevertheless, it was a wonderful flight, and I couldn't wait to really get to fly it in UPT. It was more than twice as fast as any prop aircraft I flew, and it had an ejection seat. How cool was that? Ironically, after all the cadets were through with their T-37 ride, we flew back to Rickenbacker AFB in the

KC-135, a jet I would become more familiar with after graduating from UPT.

The AFROTC summer training camp soon ended after our trip to Mississippi. I left Rickenbacker having successfully completed the course with an evaluation of high-average ranking overall. I wasn't too bothered by the evaluation result. I was just happy to be heading home so I could get back to work. I needed to pay for school, and I had taken a full month off to attend the session. The time spent in Ohio had cost me. I just had no idea how much.

So, I finished out the summer at the bakery and headed back to CSU in September. I was a little worried about finances due to my time spent in Ohio, but during my sophomore year I got a part-time job as a dishwasher at my old dorm cafeteria. They hired me back for my junior year, and this helped with daily expenses. Of course, that meant even less free time in my schedule to enjoy college life, but I was a man on a mission, anyway.

CHAPTER 4

The Chosen

So now it was the fall of 1975. More than a year had passed since the draft ended, and the Air Force was transitioning to the all-volunteer force like the other service branches. They realized they were now overmanned and were beginning to reduce the number of personnel and equipment they would retain in this post-Vietnam climate. Aircraft were grounded, as were pilots. Some pilots were not even given the opportunity to stay in the Air Force in a non-flying capacity. They were simply released back to civilian life like they were fish in a catch-and-release stream.

The AFROTC program did not escape scrutiny from the budget overlords either. Planners at headquarters were sitting down, trying to figure out how many aircraft would be needed in the future and how many pilots would be needed to fill those cockpits. The number of future aircraft did not agree with the

Some Help Along the Way

number of potential pilots already in the pipeline, so there was a dilemma that needed to be addressed and addressed quickly. At first, to solve the problem, they came to their AFROTC pilot candidates and offered them full-ride scholarships in any field other than flying. Everyone in our class with pilot slots politely declined their offer. None of us wanted to trade the wild blue yonder for the chance to end up as a missile launch officer three hundred feet underground or running the base motor pool. No, two years of free college wasn't worth that. It was a bit insulting to us that they thought it would be worth it.

So, the Air Force did next what you would expect, given the circumstances. Toward the end of the fall semester, they announced they were cutting 75 percent of the pilot training slots for our class nationwide. If you were part of the lucky 25 percent, you could sign the officer-commissioning acceptance letter and later learn when and where to report for flight training. If you were part of the 75 percent who were not going, you could choose to sign the acceptance letter and continue with the Air Force assigned to another career field. Or the other option was you could sign a different letter relieving you of any obligation to the military and walk away. Importantly for me, this option also was available to the lucky 25 percent who made the cut and would be going to UPT.

This was explained in class one day, and we were told to schedule a private conference with the professor of aerospace studies to learn our status. His name was Col. Hyde, a wonderful man in charge of a terrific staff.

We had heard rumors of the coming cuts, but the breadth and depth of those cuts were stunning even to the staff once the orders finally arrived. Everyone was shocked, including me.

At that time, to have a chance to reach a high rank, such as full colonel in an Air Force career, it was almost a requirement that you wore pilot's wings on your uniform. Being told before you were even commissioned you were not going to flight training was a serious blow to your career expectations. As I watched my fellow classmates exit the colonel's office, it was obvious to see which list they were on. Sometimes it wasn't pretty to watch.

My turn with Col. Hyde came toward the end of his list, and I was, of course, pretty anxious. He had me sit down in his office as he reviewed my pertinent Air Force records with me. Then he carefully explained the selection process, the options of remaining in the program or leaving, and the need to give the Air Force notice of my intentions. Then he laid the bombshell on me. He said I was number thirty of one hundred or so alternates to receive a UPT slot. Up until this point, no one had mentioned alternates in the equation, and he was as surprised as I was. Basically, it boiled down to the fact that if thirty of the chosen 25 percent decided to decline the offer of a pilot training slot, they could leave the Air Force without a commitment. If I in turn signed the letter saying I would accept a commission regardless of my flight-training status, I would get a UPT slot if one became available. Otherwise, I was going to be assigned to another career field and spend at least four miserable years doing something I didn't like.

Col. Hyde appreciated my predicament. Everyone else, regardless of which group they were assigned, walked out of his office with a clear choice and in charge of their future. My future was anything but clear. I either roll the dice, sign the commissioning letter, hoping against the odds that thirty of the lucky 25 percent would elect to walk away from the Air Force entirely. Or I could be the one to walk away and forget my plans for an airline career. At the time, the only realistic way to fly for the airlines was through the military. And the Air Force wasn't the only branch of the service that was experiencing a drawdown.

So, I left Col. Hyde's office feeling even more anxious than when I went in. Since my status was unclear, he urged me to take some extra time to decide which document to sign. As the colonel explained in the meeting, my academic grades were very respectable. Still, my summer camp rating kept me from being in the chosen 25 percent. What I had to determine now was the likelihood of thirty of those candidates deciding to walk away from their training slots. In my mind, it was almost inconceivable even one person would give up such a tremendous opportunity, let alone thirty. From the very beginning of our AFROTC careers at CSU, we were fed a steady diet of incredible aircraft films and briefings. We were shown what kind of maneuvers we would perform in T-37s and T-38s, including formation flying, while in flight training. We had pilots from the major commands come talk with us about their aircraft, with the intention of convincing us to make their aircraft number one on our assignment requests come assignment night at UPT. Now there was a very real chance all that opportunity for me was going to disappear.

So, as I walked around inside the AFROTC building, thinking about my dilemma and the long odds of going to UPT, once again, I heard the quiet voice. It said, "Go ahead, sign the commissioning letter. You will get your slot." It sounded just as quiet yet clear in my head as the first time I experienced it as a high school freshman telling me to join the Air Force so I could be an airline pilot. Also, when it directed me to CSU, and again, when I was walking across the campus and learning my slot was in jeopardy because of my grades. Each time I listened and complied, focusing my whole future on something that showed up unexpectedly, and I could not explain. Furthermore, I certainly could not discuss these unusual occurrences with anyone. After all, I had to pass psychological evaluations too.

So now I stood at an important crossroads. On a rational level, I thought no more than five individuals would opt out of their training slots. Honestly, I would be highly surprised if any of those fortunate twenty-five-percenters accepted the offer to walk away. Yet, here was that voice again, telling me I was going. I just had to sign the commissioning letter. This was a real test of faith in something irrational and inexplicable. I could really mess up my life if I was simply fooling myself with these silly voices that show up now and again. And really, who bases life-altering decisions on something so absurd and subjective?

Fortunately, that afternoon, I did. Against my better judgment and to the staff's surprise, I went into the administration office and signed the intent-to-commission letter half an hour after I met with Col. Hyde.

Over the years, I have reflected on that day many times. It was contrary to my nature to go against such long odds. And those odds were long by my reckoning—the equivalent of drawing two cards to complete an inside straight in poker. And the reason why was a voice in my head telling me it was okay?! You try that strategy of listening to inner voices in a poker game and you won't be at the table long. No, definitely not the smart move. A crazy move would be a better explanation.

So why did I end up taking such an outrageous gamble? The answer is it was an act of faith on my part. Faith in a God I purportedly didn't believe in but who would handle my future if I allowed him. At the time, I was unwilling to accept this. For one, pride was an issue. I had taken a few philosophy courses that changed my opinion on the existence of God, and I did quite well in them. At least, at the time, I thought I had. But with some time and reflection, I can honestly say those philosophy courses pointed out to me how shallow my faith really was. In Matthew's gospel, Jesus tells the story of the sower who sows seeds, and some fall on rocky ground. The plants wither in the sun because they can't establish deep enough roots. Well, those philosophy courses were my rocky soil, and consequently, my shallow roots of faith were exposed.

Nevertheless, I signed the letter and would live with the consequences of that decision. What made me do it? My best guess is that the roots of my faith were deeper than I thought, despite my best efforts to pull them up and get rid of them. I had a stark choice that day: ignore the voice or not. I chose not to. And that was enough for God because he had plans for me. Not that I got off easy for my detour into faithlessness. Each day I would wake up wondering if I acted capriciously, even recklessly, by signing that commitment letter. It took its toll on me. I continued to focus on my classes and studying. Still, the anxiety I left Col. Hyde's office with stayed with me the whole time.

Then, one day before my finals ended for the spring term, Capt. Mattles, one of the AFROTC instructors, knocked on my apartment door unannounced to tell me I had a UPT assignment. The quiet voice had been correct. I was going to be an Air Force pilot, after all. I cannot truly express how wonderful it was to hear this news. It was, without question, the happiest day of my young life.

Capt. Mattles provided me with some background information about the final selection outcomes while he was in the apartment. As it turned out, quite a number of AFROTC university programs didn't receive any slots for their candidates. If a program was fortunate enough to send someone to UPT, oftentimes it was just a single candidate, their distinguished AFROTC graduate. CSU sent six. Their experienced staff used their contacts and superior administrative skills to deliver handsomely for us. Had I not chosen CSU, had I not "listened" back at Rummel High School, I would not have been fortunate enough to attend UPT. I was certainly not a distinguished graduate.

I had taken a huge risk at the end of the fall term, but it paid off. I had my slot. After completing the last of my final exams the next day, I cleaned out the apartment, loaded up my Ford half-ton pickup, and headed east for Omaha. I reached home after dark, and as usual, the bakery called, wanting me to come in that night. Despite my bright future, I still had to pay for college. So, no rest for the weary, I reported for work around one o'clock in the morning, something I would get accustomed to later in life.

After spending my fourth summer working at the bakery, it was now the fall of 1976, and time to load up the truck to head back to CSU for my senior year. By now, the drive was familiar. Much of the landscape along the interstate had gently rolling hills that possessed an agrarian beauty I had come to appreciate over the years. My truck didn't even have a radio, so I was once again alone with my thoughts as I sped west toward Fort Collins. I reflected on last year at CSU and all the anguish and turmoil I experienced before the great news about UPT came the day before the school year ended. "Please," I thought to myself, "No more drama like last year. Let me just graduate, pin on my gold lieutenant bars and escape town with a diploma." My wish was granted.

I "flew" through my courses. This was so different from when I first arrived on campus. The AFROTC detachment tasked me with being the recruiting officer. So, inspired by my father, who proved throughout his advertising career that he could keep an audience's attention, I grabbed a pilot-training video from the detachment's storage room and set up a booth in the student center. It was a huge success. We had hundreds watch the show, and as it played for the crowds, I thought it would soon be me up there performing those maneuvers. Dad would have been so proud of the idea for recruitment, but I never thought to mention it to him. It was a lost opportunity I have always regretted now that he is gone.

Graduation day came. The whole class of 1977, along with their family and friends, were seated in the football stadium while the university president gave a speech. My attention was focused elsewhere, though. While the ceremony proceeded, just north of the stadium the pilot of an old WWII Stearman biplane converted to a crop duster was putting on a show of skill and daring that I found much more captivating than the speech. As far as I was concerned, it was karma. Later that day, we were commissioned in a ceremony at the AFROTC building.

A month or so earlier, those of us on flight status received our orders. I was given official notice to report to Reese Air Force

Base in Lubbock, Texas, in March of 1978. That meant I had ten months before I left home for the Lone Star State. So, I returned to the bakery, but I did use that time to earn a Federal Aviation Administration (FAA) pilot instrument rating before I showed up on base. I also sold the pickup truck and bought a brand-new Camaro with a 307-cubic-inch V-8 and a four-speed manual transmission. And, unlike my pickup, it had a radio. Interestingly, it had the same stiff ride as the pickup, but it looked and smelled much nicer.

CHAPTER 5
The Challenged

So, after leaving home in March of 1978, I drove to Lubbock, located 120 miles south of Amarillo in the Texas panhandle. The city was flat, surrounded by cotton fields and pumpjacks. The base was located west of the city, and as I approached it on that bright, sunny morning, I felt conflicted. There must have been twenty aircraft in the traffic pattern, tightly choreographed to maximize the training being done. It was electrifying for me to watch, and a part of me wanted to just pull over to the side of the road to take it all in, appreciating all the sacrifices and effort it took to bring me to that moment. For those same reasons, the other part of me couldn't imagine delaying my arrival even a minute longer. After thinking about my choice, I sped up.

I soon found myself at the entrance of the base where I received directions from the guard about where to report for my initial briefing. It didn't take long before I found myself standing among thirty-nine other young men in uniform, all with regulation haircuts like mine, and wearing well-polished shoes. Everyone in the room was trying their best not to reveal how anxious and excited they were to finally be starting flight training in this flat, windy, arid outpost of West Texas. Some managed it better than others. As for me, I didn't care if it was flat, windy, and arid outside. I had worked hard to be included in this group, qualifying for UPT by the skin of my teeth. I was grateful to be standing there and felt I had something to prove to myself. So, if this was the place I would train to earn my wings, even if it was at the far end of the earth, if not Texas, I would love it. I couldn't wait to get started, and—yes—it showed. Sometimes, though, you need to be careful about what you seek, as I would soon find out.

It would take a while to get ourselves established on base. We had to be assigned our quarters, get base parking permits, ID badges, flight suits, helmets, boots, physicals, aircraft manuals, and so much more. The only thing we lacked during our mad scramble to get settled in and collect all this equipment was the necessary time to accomplish it. We were on a tight schedule from the moment of our arrival almost to the end of the program. Our formal welcoming occurred shortly after arrival in the base auditorium, with the wing commander presiding. After introducing himself, he asked each one of us to shake hands with the person on our left and on our right. Then he intoned that by the end of the program, it was likely one of those individuals we shook hands with would not be present when the class graduated next year. In our case, it turned out he was too optimistic in his estimate.

The Challenged

The program began very well for us. By this time the class had split into two flights as we began the academic flightline portion of our training. After the split, we ended up with a terrific group of guys from all parts of the country. We were surprised to learn we even had a couple of former Vietnam vets with Army helicopter backgrounds. We were all young, highly motivated, energetic, and eager to work with one another to advance ourselves through the program. After four weeks of intense training that included lots of academic course work, parachute and ejection-seat training, and a high-altitude decompression simulation in the altitude chamber, we were sent to the aircraft flightline to begin flying the T-37, the aircraft I so looked forward to flying back in summer camp. This is also where the challenge was presented to our newly formed flight.

We were all looking forward to our first day on the aircraft flightline. After all, this flightline was the heart and soul of Undergraduate Pilot Training. It's where the rubber met the runway. The physical structures included the two large squadron buildings, one for T-37 students and one for T-38 students. Tucked between these two buildings was the huge maintenance hangar, along with some of the other smaller buildings needed for aircraft maintenance support. Base Operations, where weather briefings were obtained and flight plans were filed, was close by for easy access. Other important flightline features were the fuel depot, the fire and rescue station, and a very large concrete ramp to hold all the aircraft that were frequently coming and going over the course of the day. Finally, overlooking all of this was the aircraft control tower. The controllers staffing the tower oversaw the aircraft taxiways, runways, and the airspace around Reese up to a limited altitude.

Some Help Along the Way

When normal flight operations were up and running, the ramp was a beehive of constant activity, with numerous aircraft taxiing to and from their parking spots. Crew chiefs moved about this large concrete expanse, marshalling all these aircraft in and out of their spots while doing their best to avoid getting run over by anything with wheels or blasted by hot jet exhaust fumes. Fuel trucks moved up and down the rows of well-ordered aircraft, quickly servicing each one before their next scheduled flights. Aircraft maintenance tugs scrambled about in seemingly random fashion all over the ramp, while occasionally pulling an aircraft behind them heading to or from the maintenance hangar. Maintenance trucks would occasionally appear, elbowing their way through the constant flow of traffic when necessary to fix a less-than-flyable aircraft chocked in its parking spot. Students and their IPs (Instructor Pilots) came and went on ramp transports, responsible for getting them back and forth from the squadron building and their aircraft parking rows. And once they set foot on the ramp, it was a constant challenge for those students and their instructors to avoid all manner of hazards and vehicles as they made their way to and from the ramp transports and their aircraft. At first glance, the pace of activity seemed almost frenetic. But a closer inspection would reveal the fast-paced precision and order of a launch-and-recovery phase of flight operations that had a lot of moving parts to it. The flightline ramp was loud. It was hot. It was fast-paced. It reeked of jet-exhaust fumes, and we couldn't wait to set foot on it when the time finally arrived for our first flights in the aircraft. Until then, we would have to manage our enthusiasm and be patient just a little while longer.

So, our first day on the T-37 flightline started early in the morning as the twenty of us sat in chairs arranged around seven tables in the flight room. The sign above the door said we were in E-Flight as we marched in through the entrance earlier. It would now be our home for the next five months. We had made it this far. We had all survived the brutal reduction-in-forces cuts from a couple of years earlier, had worked hard, and made tough, personal sacrifices to be seated here this morning. We were on the cusp of piloting a twin-engine, fully aerobatic Air Force jet and our enthusiasm for the training ahead could not have been any higher. Now we were eager to see who our instructors would be.

We had no warning about what was to happen next as the instructors marched in. The room was called to attention by our flight leader. We responded by standing up in unison and snapping into those feet together, hands at our sides, chests out, shoulders back, rigid military postures we all had drilled into us by now. The IPs marched around the perimeter of our modest-sized, square-shaped flight room to their students' tables, pivoted toward these fresh new faces, and waited for the command to salute. The command was given, and we saluted them, doing a pretty good job for a group of mostly AFROTC graduates. They returned our salute and that turned out to be the high point of our class relationship with the instructor pilots of E-Flight.

We were threatened and harangued for the next hour or so, each instructor getting his turn, culminating with our flight commander proclaiming he felt it was his job to wash as many of us out as possible. He sounded sincere, and he was. This wasn't a determined effort by the instructor corps of E-Flight to initially break down their students so they could build them back into the pilots the Air Force required. Rather, it was a determined effort to break them down so they could be disposed of, the sooner the better. At least I have to credit our flight commander for his honesty. He let us know it was coming.

So, it was not quite the first day on the flightline we were anticipating, as we silently took all this in. Instead, as our flight commander was finishing up his introductory remarks, it was dawning on us that we just heard the opening bell for the twelve-round prize fight our lives were about to become. What's more, he and his team of instructors had just landed the first punch. I must admit, they caught us flat-footed that morning. We certainly weren't expecting to be threatened with broken limbs from our flight-scheduling officer for failing to correctly annotate his scheduling board after returning from a flight. Nor were we expecting from another instructor a rant describing the ruin that would befall a student who failed to report to his instructor on time for a flight briefing, or without his gradebook in hand, and not showing proper obeisance to both. Each of our new instructor pilots addressed us that morning and not one of them managed to offer a warm welcome or even some words of encouragement as we were about to start the flying phase of the program. It wasn't just unsettling. It bordered on being bizarre.

To make matters worse, we soon got to know students in other flights, and they were experiencing nothing like what we were going through. Same curriculum. Same building. But two different worlds as far as approaches to instructing students. To us, it felt as if salt were being rubbed into the wound. Had we been sitting in one room to the left or right of us that morning, we would not be engaged in such an intense, pugilistic struggle just to keep our seats in the flight room and our futures in the

Air Force. The one significant positive development that came from our introductory flightline briefing that morning was its effect on our attitude as a flight. It united us in a mutual dislike of them that only worsened as the program progressed. This was unfortunate because the training was already demanding enough without the added pressure of flight instructors very willing to send you out the gate with your bags. We lost some good candidates unnecessarily.

It was no surprise then that the next five months turned out to be the hardest, most-challenging period in my life, and I suspect for many of my classmates, it was the same as well. The course syllabus seemed to be built on the premise there were more than twenty-four hours in a student-pilot's day. We had academic courses in applied aerodynamics, meteorology, flight planning, navigation, aircraft systems, and more, all of which required diligent study for the written test at the end of each course. We needed to spend numerous hours in the building's learning center. There we would view slide shows from the center's voluminous library of circular carousels on such topics as the exterior inspection of the T-37 or visual landmarks for navigating to or from the practice areas. This was not exactly riveting material to watch, but it was nonetheless vital to success in the program. We had to prepare, then perform for our sessions in the T-37 procedural trainers. Here we would be tested on such skills as the proper way to perform the initial cockpit setup for the aircraft or the execution of normal flight checklists. We were scheduled for sessions in full-motion simulators to not only develop our instrument crosscheck skills but also practice emergency procedures and judgment in a realistic-appearing environment. We were given sheet after sheet of study materials filled with numbers and procedures.

They all needed to be memorized to the point where you could recite them back in your sleep if you wanted to remain in the program.

All this preparation and practice on the ground was enough to make your head explode from the sheer amount of knowledge needed to be quickly crammed into it. And by now we were flying the airplane too. The pace of the program was pedal-to-the-metal fast. If you got behind on any of your syllabus training, there was a very real possibility you would never catch up. To make sure we stayed motivated to keep up with the pace, we were informed that more than two failures of academic written tests meant dismissal from the program. Check-ride failures in the airplane or the simulator were equally as harsh. You would be given one review ride, then a recheck. Fail that and you get a final check ride. Fail that and you were packing your bags. The program was designed to eliminate any stragglers and was brutally efficient in its implementation. None of us wanted to be stragglers. Consequently, our days were filled with activities, and our nights were full of study and preparation.

Our days usually started early with us standing at attention in the flight room. After being allowed to sit, we would be briefed on any flightline topic of interest or concern, followed by stand-up emergency procedures—"stand-ups" for short. For stand-ups, a lucky student would be called to attention and then given a flight scenario that tested his knowledge of aircraft systems, procedures, limitations, and judgment. Properly done, it could prove invaluable in enhancing group knowledge, increasing the students' confidence in their training, and improving their capabilities in the aircraft. It could even provide an opportunity to inject some humor into an early morning before the rapid pace of our day began. Many of our E-Flight IPs instead used this as a platform for sarcasm and ridicule, their preferred method of instruction. It was done with the unmistakable air of malevolence that buttressed our flight commander's welcoming address. Needless to say, this did not endear them to us.

One thing we all quickly learned during our first days on the flightline was that Undergraduate Pilot Training was built around the course syllabus. Each event in the syllabus—whether it was an academic course, a stint in the T-37 procedural trainer, a trip to the flight simulator, or an actual flight in the aircraft—had objectives to achieve. Master the skill or objective required in the syllabus and a rectangular box was darkened with a pencil on a computer grade sheet. Results were then sent off to be filed on a computer program somewhere while you moved on to the next objective. The syllabus was designed with enough objectives in the program to keep a student very busy for a year.

We also learned the syllabus was designed to be implemented at only one speed: flat-out. Unless you were completely committed to this year-long sprint, you were likely to be one of those students spoken about by the wing commander during his arrival address who wasn't present when the class graduated. To succeed, you needed to embrace the attitude you were either going to make it through the program or you were going to die trying. Any level of commitment less than that and your success was questionable—at least it was in our flight. Out of necessity, I tried to focus on just making it through the day, doing my best to meet the challenges each day presented. I certainly didn't have to fight off boredom as I slowly made my way through the T-37 program, one day at a time.

If your first syllabus event of the day was scheduled to be a flight, you would report to your assigned instructor, gradebook in hand, for the pre-flight briefing. The gradebook would be reviewed, then the syllabus would be referenced for the required events to be briefed. Some events, such as recovering from a spin using the single-spin recovery procedure or flying your way out of a fully configured landing stall, involved a greater level of in-flight preparation before they could be executed. Therefore, they needed to be thoroughly discussed and planned before you left the building. Moreover, you couldn't remain in the practice area for as long as you sometimes needed to master the skill demanded by the syllabus. The T-37 was designed for an hour-and-a-half mission, and unless you were the last flight of the day for that sector, someone was scheduled to come in behind you in your practice area. Consequently, a plan was needed to maximize the training being done with the limited time we had in both the aircraft and the practice area. It soon became apparent to us that the syllabus was a demanding taskmaster, and we all were becoming slaves to it. Even solo flights could have a challenging list of objectives.

After all the briefing questions were answered, the IP and the student would soon meet in the life-support room, where they would collect their parachutes and helmets. After a few checks of their equipment, they would exit the squadron building, grab seats on the ramp transport, and ride out to their aircraft parking row. Once they were airborne, normally a very short flight over to the auxiliary field was done to practice touch-and-go landings, followed by a trip into an area assigned by ATC (air traffic control) to perform the flight maneuvers called for in the syllabus.

When the maneuvers were completed, the student would

again contact ATC for clearance to exit the area and pick up the visual arrival back to Reese for a full-stop landing. Clear the runway, taxi to your parking spot, shut down the engines, complete the checklists and aircraft forms — then it's back on the ramp transport for a return ride to the squadron building. Once inside, we would hang up our parachutes and helmet bags in life support before we would debrief the flight back at our IP's table. It took approximately three hours from start to finish, and between the withering heat of the West Texas summer, the physical stress of the aerobatic maneuvers (coupled with the mental stress imposed by our IPs), we came back to the flight room both fatigued and dehydrated. The routine was highly scripted, and it was a good thing we were all young because oftentimes we did this twice a day.

When I first arrived in Lubbock, I was confident I would do well. I already knew how to handle an airplane and to better prepare myself for the training, I had just finished earning my FAA instrument rating. I was twenty-three years old, single, and about to fly jets for the Air Force. I had a life almost anyone would envy, but I would soon be reminded how pride always goes before the fall.

I ran into an unexpected problem with my initial flights in the T-37. Although I came to Reese AFB with a few hundred hours of flying time, I wasn't familiar with the aerobatic maneuvers, and flying upside down was causing me to experience airsickness. This occurred enough for the flight surgeon to warn me that the next time it happened would be my last flight in pilot training. My IP was made aware of it, and now I was a marked man. Between the airsickness and our flight commander's address to us on our first day on the flightline, it was going to take a miracle to keep me in the program.

Fortunately for me, I managed to clean up my act in the airplane. I guess I needed to be threatened with elimination to get serious about flying upside down. My IP was watching me closely during the following flights, hoping to catch me get queasy enough so he could send me out of the gate with my bags. We hadn't exactly developed a close bond of mutual respect and friendship since our class came to the flightline, and in his mind, it was only a matter of time before I would be gone. The miracle for me came in the form of a pink liquid I purchased at the base exchange. Before each flight, I would enter the men's room and surreptitiously down a few swallows of Pepto Bismol from the bottle I hid in my helmet bag. It worked. Now I was starting to honestly enjoy aerobatics. Pepto Bismol was changing my world, especially when I was looking down at it through the top of the aircraft canopy.

By this time our class was approaching the point in the program where we were to fly our first solo in the T-37. It would just be a simple pattern ride, taking off from the T-37 departure runway at Reese, pulling up into the visual traffic pattern and performing five to seven touch-and-go landings before full-stopping the aircraft and taxiing back to the ramp. To celebrate the event, all your classmates participated in very unceremoniously throwing you in a horse tank filled with water located just outside the entrance to the squadron building. No one would bother to change their flight suit after their flight-training "baptism." It would continue to be worn by the solo student as a damp badge of honor for the day's noteworthy achievement. After all, not everyone gets to fly an Air Force jet solo.

Yet even though the student is flying solo in the pattern, he needs to be monitored and graded, so this responsibility falls on the supervisor of flying (SOF). The SOF is an IP who sits in a small, square, custom-made trailer designed with four large tinted windows for a 360-degree view and, mercifully, is air-conditioned. He sits, along with a student-pilot aide, in the trailer parked between runways, monitoring all aircraft in his pattern. He acts as the control tower, clearing students for takeoffs, touch-and-go landings, full-stops, go-arounds, or even directs them to break out of the traffic pattern if it gets too full. He is also called upon to grade the overall performance of solo students flying in his traffic pattern. The grade would be radioed in from the trailer to the front desk of the squadron building, and students would pick up the form with their grades after their flights. Acting as a SOF is an important but thankless job at a UPT base.

So, my IP and I flew the pre-solo flight, going to the auxiliary field close by for a few touch-and-go landings, then headed to our assigned area to practice aircraft stalls, followed by a spin recovery. We left the area, picked up the visual arrival back at Reese, and did an overhead pattern to a full stop. We taxied back to the ramp, parked the airplane, shut down the engines, and headed back to E-Flight to debrief. It was a good flight. The Pepto Bismol was working, and there were no issues with my performance. My IP filled out the computer grade sheet as satisfactory overall and filed it.

I felt a slight sense of relief after our debrief. I had passed the pre-solo ride, and tomorrow I would be alone in the cockpit when I pushed up the throttles for takeoff. It was certainly going to be enjoyable leaving on the ground all that extra weight that ordinarily sat next to me as I released the brakes. But mostly,

I expected tomorrow's flight to be anticlimactic. For one, it wouldn't be my first time alone in the cockpit. The bigger concern for me was what price was I paying for the privilege? Around this time, someone mentioned there were three ways to fly an airplane: the right way, the wrong way, and the Air Force way. Was all the intimidation, harassment, and humiliation our flight experienced from the staff piled on top of the very real danger of training for a combat environment the Air Force way to fly? Apparently, no other flight in the squadron building felt it was. If this were the case, then where were the grownups in the squadron to correct this misuse of resources? There are tremendous monetary costs involved in training a student candidate to become an Air Force pilot. Entire bases were created, supplied, and staffed to train the best candidates the Air Force could provide. And the candidates themselves paid a heavy price in personal sacrifice. Sometimes they even paid with their lives.

Why, then, would a rogue flight commander be allowed to waste all this time, money, and talent by doing his best to empty his flight room of students? I had no answers. I just knew the oversight was sorely needed in our case but somehow was overlooked as we struggled through the T-37 curriculum. That was about all the time I could afford to reflect on our unique circumstances within the squadron. I needed to prepare for tomorrow. I could only surmise my fellow E-Flight classmates and I were all born under the wrong star and now were collectively paying the price for it. We would just have to get ourselves through T-37s without any adult supervision, and for me that meant doing it one day at a time.

There was a lot of energy and excitement in the flight room the next morning. Quite a few of us, me included, were listed on the scheduling board as first solos. It was an important milestone in the program, and it required you to get your IP's signature on a short form acknowledging you were to solo the jet with his blessing. I caught him as he was getting ready to leave the flight room and presented it to him. He looked at the form and became apoplectic. He shouted at me, "You can't solo! I won't allow it!"

I was caught completely off guard by his reaction. We had had a good flight the previous afternoon. "What on earth is going through his mind?" I thought as I stood there, trying to come up with a response to his angry backlash at my request. After a couple of seconds, I just responded by saying, "The syllabus has me up for it." It was at this point he realized he was completely hemmed in by his own doing. He couldn't retrieve the computer grade sheet from the previous flight and change the grade to unsatisfactory. If he could, he most certainly would. But by now, it was beyond his grasp and so was his ability to control the situation. His eyes frantically searched around the room as if trying to find an escape from his circumstances hidden within its confines. But the search was pointless, and he realized it. His eyes finally settled on the form I was holding. He ended up quickly grabbing it out of my hand, signing it, and thrusting it back at me. He followed this with some awful words I have never forgotten and probably never will, turned, and stomped out of the room.

It proved to be a pivotal moment in the program for me. After a few seconds' pause to collect myself, I left the flight room, found my aircraft parking spot written on a board behind the front desk of the squadron building, then went to collect my helmet and parachute. I didn't need a side trip to the men's room for some Pepto Bismol, nor would I ever need it again. That focus and resolve I experienced my sophomore year of college after learning my UPT slot was in jeopardy due to grades was, once again, flooding through me. I went out, flew the pattern solo flight, and returned to E-Flight. One of our E-Flight instructors was the SOF during my solo, and he graded my flight as "excellent." I slid his grade form across the table to my instructor without a word. He read the grade, turned his gaze away from both me and that small sheet of paper, and chose not to utter a single word. Some response on his part. Muted as it was though, it was enough of a response for me. Both of us knew it wasn't going to be a simple matter for him to eliminate me from training now. The preliminary rounds were over, and no knockout punch had been thrown. It looked like this fight was going the full twelve rounds.

Most of us, at some point, struggled while learning to fly the T-37 "the Air Force way," trying to keep our heads above water while the pace of the syllabus and our IPs did their best to pull us under. Those who were better swimmers reached out a helping hand to those of us flailing in the deep end, and by doing so, saved a number of us from drowning. I guess those unselfish acts on their part proved vexing for our flight commander. One morning during the daily briefing, he introduced an exercise that called for your fellow tablemates to point out to the rest of the flight the most egregious error of flying you made during the week. It occurred to me as we were listening to him that this exercise was just a thinly disguised attempt to sow disunity among classmates. You didn't need a degree in psychology to come to that conclusion, and the more he spoke about the exercise, the less appealing it sounded. No one liked what they were hearing from him. Unfortunately, he was in charge, so we were going to engage in his exercise, regardless of what we thought of it.

So, we all "engaged" in the exercise that morning, but we certainly didn't embrace it. As the shaming went from table to table, there were very few enthusiastic recountings of screwups by fellow classmates that our flight commander was hoping for. Most were dispirited recollections of events that were hardly egregious and merely offered to move the exercise along to its awkward conclusion. When our table was up, neither of my tablemates said anything, and I just self-reported a minor checklist aberration during a solo flight.

Not surprisingly, our flight commander's attempt to introduce a little discord between us fell flat. We were never asked to engage in the "snitch" exercise again, and we remained strongly unified throughout our time at Reese. But it didn't stop him and his staff from continuing to try to separate us, always probing for weakness. We could never let our guard down. By the time our training in the T-37 was over, we had battled them to a stalemate. Those of us left standing at the end had survived because we looked out for each other and offered a helping hand when needed. It took just about everything we had to survive the experience, leaving us shell-shocked. We stumbled into our T-38 training like we had just left a war zone. As far as we were concerned, we had.

So, we moved down the ramp to a twin building that contained the T-38 flight rooms, and once again, we were in E-Flight. Fortunately, this would be the only similarity between the two programs.

The first three days, we were all quiet and subdued, even tentative, as we shuffled about the flight room trying to prepare for training on this new aircraft. We had left a terrible situation and were so mentally beaten up by the experience it hardly occurred to us that this might not be a reprise of our T-37 past, where fear and intimidation became the foundation of our training. It got to the point our new flight commander, Capt. Paul Schwemler, addressed us to ask what was wrong. He and the rest of his instructors had never seen any prior class act like this. There were no smiles being displayed, no jokes, or pranks being played, no laughter or enthusiasm being shown by any of us. They were completely flummoxed by what they were seeing. We just stared back at him in silence, expecting the hammer to drop the instant we let our guard down. It was a very sad moment but understandable considering where we just came from.

Later that day, my T-38 instructor pilot and flight scheduling officer, Capt. Reece, informed my tablemate and me that we would soon have a new instructor. He was separating from the Air Force so he could embark on a new career with Braniff Airlines. He wasn't sure yet who would be taking his place, but at that moment, he wasn't too concerned about it. He decided he would much rather talk about the indignities he suffered at the hands of the Air Force, and we were his audience. Someone interrupted his diatribe to ask a scheduling question, and that was all it took. Now he was up and complaining loud enough for everyone in the flight room to hear. Our new flight commander came out of his office and, in an equally loud voice, said, "F—k off, Reece!" It was an epiphany for all of us there. For one, our former instructor pilots were mostly a collection of maladjusted religious zealots who not only were narrow-minded and unforgiving, but would never talk like that, especially in front of us.

We looked at each other, then felt a huge wave of relief washing over us as it filled the room. We realized, at that moment, we had put our T-37 experience behind us. No more acting as if we were walking on eggshells with this move down the ramp. Now it was time to fly the T-38, and this time our instructors were there to challenge us to get better, not kick us to the curb.

What a change in attitude it was for us. Going from trying to avoid even the slightest mistake lest you get hammered in the debrief to an attitude of testing the boundaries and accepting some mistakes will be made in the process.

This new attitude was perfectly illustrated by the training we received when we started formation flying in the T-38. The formation wingman would be sent out from a tight wingtip position (three feet clearance) to a trailing position (one mile behind) from the lead aircraft. Then he would be signaled to rejoin the wingtip position, usually by the lead ship rocking his wings.

The rejoin was done generally with one hundred knots of overtake, and sometimes the wingman would overshoot the lead as we all tried to rejoin as quickly as possible. The attitude instilled in us about how aggressively we should rejoin was summed up by our IPs' admonition, "If you are not overshooting one out of four times on your rejoins, you're not being aggressive enough!" When we heard this, it felt as if we were being unshackled from our T-37 past, where tolerance for error was severely limited. Here in the T-38, aggressiveness was being encouraged, and it was just what we needed to hear.

Many of those rejoins took place at well above one hundred knots of overtake just to exercise those "aggressiveness" muscles that had been neglected for so long.

Yet it would be misleading if you were to think this was suddenly an easy program. Hardly. The T-38 was a much faster aircraft with completely different flying characteristics. We had to think and respond faster. We still had stand-up EPs (Emergency Procedures) with our daily flight briefings. We still had academics and simulators, and everything was graded. But now we looked forward to it. There was nothing else we would rather do or any place else on earth we would rather be. Frequently we would get to fly twice a day, and we especially looked forward to formation flying. Now we would oftentimes respond to one another with an incredulous, "Can you believe it! We're getting PAID to do this s—t!" as we went through our day. That enthusiasm for training we lost our first day of the T-37 flightline was being rediscovered here in T-38s. What a complete turnaround in attitude it was for our flight.

That change in attitude was reflected in our learning and progress. Using me as an example, I started the flightline the same way I started college—that is, with difficulty. I "busted" my T-37 contact check (visual flying plus aerobatics) and simulator instrument check (weather flying). This was really not a good start, especially for someone who came in with some flying experience. To make matters worse, I quickly failed two academic tests, putting me in jeopardy of elimination. After our T-37 flight commander's address the first day, I rightly felt like I had a target on my back as I went through the program. But with maximum effort, I made it through the flying gauntlet they fashioned their program into.

With the move down the street to the T-38 building and a more enlightened instructor crew, I scored "excellent" in contact flying, "excellent" in formation, and "good" in navigation (cross-country) flying. Moreover, no one in our flight busted a check ride. As far as anyone in the squadron could recall, this was unprecedented. But I am getting ahead of myself again. Let me take a few steps back.

With our newfound confidence and change in attitude, we were tearing up the program in T-38s. We still had each other's backs on and off base and shared everything to help each other advance. As graduation approached, we received a form to fill out to request our aircraft assignment. It was referred to as a "dream sheet." You pick three aircraft in ranked order, and on assignment night, in front of just about the whole flying wing gathered at the Officer's Club to listen and drink, you find out what it will be.

A lot of thought and speculation goes into filling out the form. After all, it is your post-graduation life, and I was thinking about an airline career. So, I filled it out with heavy aircraft in mind, avoiding the Strategic Air Command (SAC) entirely. I needed to build flying time to pursue an airline career. SAC famously sat on alert for seven-day stretches and flew just enough to stay minimally qualified. If you were a man with a family to raise, SAC was a good choice because you were home more often than other Air Force pilots and could have some contact with your wife and children while serving on alert. But in my case, I was definitely not a man with a family. SAC just didn't fit in with the future I envisioned for myself. So, we all filled out the forms and submitted them to Management Personnel Center, MPC for short. Then we waited for that day when our names would be called at the Officer's Club, and we would each stand up in front of everyone to learn our fate.

But that was about six weeks away, and we still had much to do in the meantime. More flying, more simulators, more quizzes, and stand-up EPs to fill in the time between now and then. But honestly, we were like kids waiting for Christmas to arrive.

During this time, I found myself sitting alone, looking at a big map of the United States under some clear plexiglass covering the top of our instructor's briefing table. As I looked at the map, I began to wonder where I might end up after assignment night. After all, as the map showed, it was a big country with quite a number of bases located throughout all fifty states.

That's assuming I was stationed stateside. I couldn't rule out the possibility of being stationed overseas, either. As this was all going through my mind, I heard the quiet voice again. I was told I would be given a KC-135 based in the Northern Tier. I was momentarily stunned by this new revelation, even though you would think I would be used to it by now. After all, this was the fifth time it had happened to me, the first experience occurring nine years earlier. This time, however, that stunned reaction was followed by a sinking feeling in my stomach, as if I had stepped off the edge of a cliff. If the quiet voice was right, my career plans might be in jeopardy. SAC pilots flew very little compared to the other Air Force Commands. How was I going to log sufficient flying time to leave the Air Force and be competitive in the airline job market? If this occasional, elucidative voice wanted me flying the friendly skies, SAC was not the way to go. A better alternative was the Military Airlift Command (MAC), with its massive fleet of cargo and transport aircraft. Besides, SAC was no fun, and I had no desire to be stationed in some remote area near the Canadian border, which was the defining feature of Northern Tier bases.

Yet, even as all this was racing through my mind, I sensed this would soon become a reality, and I might as well resign myself to it. The quiet voice hadn't misled me so far. Despite my misgivings, I should trust it would all work out. Unfortunately, that wasn't my response. Rather than trust what I heard that day, I did my best just to put it out of my mind. If the voice was right, I couldn't see how this would play out successfully. If the voice was wrong and I ended up elsewhere, have I just been fooling myself all these years? I guess I would have to wait to learn the answer.

Assignment night finally arrived. I flew a four-ship formation flight in the late afternoon with our flight commander, Capt. Schwemler, as my IP, debriefed the sortie quickly, and headed over to the Officer's Club. The big ceremony room had already been set up with chairs in the center for our class, along with a big projector screen to display pictures of the aircraft we would be assigned as they announced where we would be stationed. The sides of the room were already filling up with IPs and students of other flights waiting to hear the results, and alcohol was definitely being served.

Our class took their seats as they filtered in, and shortly after we all were present, the ceremony began. These were always raucous affairs, and the O' Club bar always had a good night whenever they occurred. Still, this particular assignment night was louder and more boisterous than usual. The list of assignments announced was not impressive, and the bystanders let our class know it in no uncertain terms. My name was called about two-thirds of the way through the list, and I stood up, hoping not to hear what I expected. The master of ceremonies announced my three aircraft requests from the dream sheet. He then pressed a button on his handheld device to display a big picture of a KC-135 on the screen and said, "You're assigned a KC-135 to Grand Forks Air Force Base." I think I earned the biggest collective groan for the night from those beer-fueled bystanders. I was in a state of momentary shock. Since my latest voice experience, assignment night was no longer just about my assignment. I heard I would be flying tankers, but I was a little unsure about the rest. I turned to my buddy and asked, "Did he say Grand Forks?" With a look of sympathy, he said yes, and now it was my turn to groan.

CHAPTER 6

"Did he say Grand Forks?"

A s I suspected, the quiet voice proved prescient. Grand Forks AFB is located five hundred miles due north of Omaha in North Dakota and about a stone's throw away from the Canadian border.

It was a tough night for me. Rather than being grateful to learn I had an incredible ally in my corner looking out for me, I was deeply disappointed in my assignment selection. Talk about missing the forest for the trees. I was focused on how hard I worked to get into UPT and all the effort it took to get this far in the program. Nobody expended more effort than me in doing either. Yet, in the end, it was a plane I didn't want in a place I didn't want to be. It must have shown on my face because after the ceremony, a couple of classmates told me they could understand if I started drinking that night. I was too disappointed to reply, so I just nodded my head but, of course, that didn't happen. The one piece of good news I heard was Grand Forks had T-38s for copilots to fly when they weren't flying the bomber or the tanker. That news helped ease the disappointment somewhat.

But our time together as a class was soon coming to an end. The last major event to challenge us was the navigation check. For this event, we would reach into essentially a bingo cage and pick out a numbered ball associated with an Air Force base and a profile to fly. We would have to plan, then fly the profile to the selected base from the back seat of the T-38 under a canopy hood while the evaluator pilot sat up front, monitoring visually outside and our performance on instruments from the inside. This experience was the program's culmination for us, and some profiles were harder than others. Near the start of the navigation check for our flight, one of our guys drew out the easiest profile ball from the cage, and rather than return the ball, he palmed it. So, the following three or four navigation checks came up with the same profile, a truly remarkable coincidence. Unfortunately, by the time I was ready for the navigation check, the remarkable profile ball had been returned to the cage. I did fine on the check ride, flying a different profile, but as I wrote earlier, we had each other's backs, on and off base and to the very end.

Shortly afterward, it was time to say goodbye to Lubbock, Texas, and some wonderful people who became lifelong friends. Capt. Schwemler, in his farewell address, told us how remarkable our flight's perfect record of check-ride success was (if only he knew), and he also shared something else. Our T-37 flight commander had contacted him to arrange for our training records to be transferred to him as we arrived. Our former flight commander told him that as a group we were weak but wished him good luck, the implication being he would need it.

After all we had undergone in both T-37s and T-38s, it was remarkable to hear this as we were heading out the door for the last time. We had met the challenge from our old nemesis in T-37s and were left standing in the end, all successful with Air Force wings pinned on our uniforms. We had gone from "weak" to perfect. It proves how critical leadership is with people and their endeavors. But it also points out how important forgiveness is "toward those who speak ill of you," which, at the moment, wasn't something I was very willing to do. It would take more time and maturity on my part.

So, Mom and Dad drove from Omaha to Lubbock to be at the graduation ceremony and see us all receive our wings. Their attitude about me joining the Air Force had changed from when I first told them my plans years ago in high school. They now also knew what a KC-135 was and had an idea of where Grand Forks was located.

I was able to make a quick trip home before I had to report to Castle Air Force Base in central California for four months of training to fly the KC-135. I was somewhat surprised the bakery didn't call asking if I was home yet. Soon enough, though, I was heading west in my Camaro to undergo more training and to transition from flying a small, speedy, highly maneuverable fighter-type trainer, to a huge, lumbering Boeing 707 with a crew of four. It would take a while.

After Castle Air Force Base, I was officially christened a SAC KC-135 copilot and sent on my way to Grand Forks. I was driving east and driving fast this time because I had to report to Grand Forks in three days. I barely made it, but I did have enough time to clean myself up before I reported to my new squadron. As my father said, "You only have one chance to make a good first impression." Funny how fathers get smarter as one grows older. It was certainly true in my case.

CHAPTER 7
Joel Schrimsher

Getting settled in the squadron took some time. One of the impressions I developed at Castle AFB when I arrived was the Strategic Air Command didn't move quickly on just about anything. It was true here in Grand Forks as well. After receiving my Top Secret clearance, I had to report to the secure room in the alert facility to learn the mission. After what seemed to be an interminable amount of time and study, I was certified to serve as a crewmember on alert and assigned to a crew. Finally, I was at the end of the training pipeline. And almost like a reward for my efforts, I was allowed to fly the T-38 again.

Yet, climbing back into the T-38 wasn't quite as simple as I had hoped. This wonderful, new opportunity I was so looking forward to had restrictions. I couldn't simply show up in my flight suit with my helmet bag in hand and expect to jump into the cockpit of the "White Rocket." It required a formal checkout, and the checkout process began with a form requiring the signature of my KC-135 squadron commander. The form was at the T-38 detachment commander's office, inside a huge old hangar originally built to shelter F-106 interceptors and their mechanics.

I left the alert facility after I completed the mission-certification briefing and sped directly over to the T-38 office to collect the form. I was anxious to get the process started right away. In my mind, this would be the single silver lining in the dark cloud that had settled over my outlook since assignment night back at Reese AFB. Now that I was certified as a member of the Alert Crew Force, life was about to change dramatically. Every third week would be spent tied to the alert compound and our mission aircraft. Moreover, I learned just how little flying time in the tanker I could expect every month. If I was planning to leave the Air Force before I turned thirty years old and have a shot at flying for a major carrier, I would need more flying time. In other words, my career plans would depend on my involvement in the Accelerated Co-pilot Enrichment program (ACE) and the T-38.

I parked my Camaro by the hangar's office door and after exiting the car, stepped inside the building. As I stepped into the office, I hoped to quickly collect the form, race over to the tanker squadron, and obtain my squadron commander's signature. With a little luck, I might be back in the front cockpit of the T-38 by tomorrow morning. It turns out I was stepping into more than just the detachment's office.

It seemed like a lifetime ago, but I had met the T-38 ACE detachment commander before. Seeing him reminded me of the circumstances. Back at Reese when we were preparing for our navigation check rides, the head of the check section (i.e., chief evaluator pilot for student check rides) came into our flight room to give us the formal briefing. He brought with him the bingo cage I mentioned earlier, which contained the numbered balls that determined our check-ride profiles. He outlined how the check ride would proceed and talked about the standards of performance his staff expected to see from us. He answered all our questions, tucked the bingo cage under his arm, and as he was leaving, said he wouldn't be evaluating any of our check rides personally. He was departing soon for his new assignment as the T-38 ACE detachment commander of Grand Forks. Then he added cavalierly, "I expect to see a few of you up there soon" as he headed out the door.

Back then, neither of us knew his prediction would be fulfilled on assignment night when I stood up. We also didn't know how important a role he would play in my life both at Grand Forks and after I left the Air Force.

But none of that mattered at the moment. Our second meeting took place under very different circumstances. As I entered the office area, Capt. Joel Schrimsher, former chief of check section at Reese AFB, was seated behind his Air Force standard-issue, gray metal desk. He didn't bother to get up. He had an attractive, young female airman on his lap, and considering his past dealings with new crewmembers assigned to the wing, he didn't look happy to see me, anyway. He knew the instant I came through the doorway why I was there. I was just another SAC 2nd Lt. copilot looking to fly his airplanes. He had already seen enough of us to know what to expect, and it wasn't much.

Nevertheless, I went through the ritual, introducing myself, asking questions about the ACE program, and doing my best to ignore the major breach of officer-enlisted etiquette sitting on his lap. He didn't move from his chair and tried to get rid of me like he would a bothersome fly. I could understand his motivation. Besides being a lanky, twenty-four-year-old 2nd Lt., a rank universally disliked by the officer and enlisted corps, the young airman really was quite attractive. But I wasn't leaving until I had my questions answered and the paperwork in hand to enroll in the program.

Joel can be an intimidating fellow. And sarcastic. He was a helicopter pilot in Vietnam assigned to fly rescue missions, so he was also fearless. I guess I was showing more backbone than he had come to expect from previous encounters with new applicants to the program. At some point, I passed the threshold he had set to enlist his cooperation, and the temperature in the room suddenly changed. The female airman was off his lap and out the door. I had the necessary enrollment form in hand, and we were working on scheduling my first flight.

What a difference persistence can make. I hadn't flown with Joel yet, but I passed his first test. I showed I wasn't easily intimidated by him, which was critically important in his mind because he was responsible for the airplanes he was assigned. If I couldn't stand up to a little intimidation inflicted by him in his office, how would I respond in the airplane when there was a mechanical or weather issue, maybe both? Would I get overwhelmed by the situation, or could I maintain my focus? He needed to know what kind of pilot he was loaning his airplane to fly. Like I said earlier, I hadn't flown with him yet, but at least I had shown him some potential.

I wasn't able to get back into the cockpit of the T-38 the next day. I couldn't get my squadron commander's signature on the enrollment form as quickly as I had hoped. The delay proved helpful, though. It allowed me time to review the aircraft's systems, procedures, performance limits, and more. I wouldn't be completely unfamiliar with the airplane when I was finally allowed to climb back into the cockpit. By that time, it would be almost a year since my last flight, and a lot had changed. For one thing, I would now be responsible for knowing two aircraft well enough to bet my wings each time I flew them. I also understood if I were unfortunate enough to bend one of Joel's airplanes, losing my wings, unfortunate as that might be, would not be my primary concern.

CHAPTER 8
Crewed Up and Screwed Up

My first crew assignment turned out to be very fortunate. I had a wonderful, patient man as crew commander who was also an instructor pilot in the tanker. The major benefit of that was you were allowed to do touch-and-go landings. Regulations stated that if an IP was not in one of the two front seats, you were allowed to make low approaches; otherwise, all landings were full stops. Most of our missions were planned with some extra pattern time for the pilots, so I was able to gain more experience in landings than otherwise. This was soon to prove providential for me.

Let me explain the T-38 being stationed way up in North Dakota, a highly unlikely spot for such a warm-weather airplane. They were on loan to the Strategic Air Command because SAC pilots didn't fly much. Their mission was to sit on alert in the base alert facility and be ready at a moment's notice to fly in the event of a nuclear attack by our enemies. The pilots flew just enough to stay minimally qualified for that attack scenario. Naturally, their flying skills suffered, and flying time was essential for a copilot to upgrade to aircraft commander. The T-38 provided a relatively cheap, excellent way to gain the time and experience necessary for moving into the left seat. For me, it was a godsend in so many ways. For one, it convinced me I got the best assignment of our group on assignment night, even with North Dakota winters.

So now let me return to my position as a new tanker copilot in the squadron. Life was going well enough. I was getting more comfortable in the tanker, and flying the T-38 in my free time helped improve my aeronautical skills. I was twenty-five years old, gaining confidence and hitting my stride, when my aircraft commander told me he was being transferred to a desk job to help him get promoted. A new man would replace him on the crew. Unfortunately, the new man wasn't an IP yet, so there would be no more touch-and-go landings in the tanker. I hated to see him go because he was a wonderful man and a good mentor, but I understood the need for promotion. Now I had to just wait and see who would fill his shoes. The answer to that question soon followed.

Not everyone shared my enthusiasm for Grand Forks and the beautiful T-38s parked on the base's ramp. To provide context, the Air Force realized it had made a serious mistake in assessing the number of pilots it would need back when I was in college. A massive defense buildup under President Reagan forced their analysts to throw away the old plans and start fresh with much larger figures. With new numbers now in hand, they found themselves scrambling to fill their cockpits. We had a pilot-retention briefing held in the alert facility, of all places, to hear from one of these analysts. During his presentation, he said it took an average of twelve pilot departures from the Air Force before one aircraft commander from a southern base would accept an assignment to North Dakota. By this time, many Air Force pilots who could were headed for the airlines, and those on the fence about staying in had an easy time deciding if they were assigned to Grand Forks. Those aircraft commanders already trapped there paid the price with additional time sitting on alert. Sometimes transfers were delayed because they couldn't find replacements. Consequently, morale suffered.

Our new aircraft commander arrived fresh from the halls of academia, where he had been pursuing a doctorate in geology. Unfortunately, he was unable to complete his degree because he was needed up here. He was obviously smart, yet he had been out of the cockpit a while. He brought his family with him, a wife and six children, so obviously Catholic. He went through the local checkout program, and we had one flight as a crew before we were scheduled to deploy to California to support an exercise. He was a very nice and generous man who would give you the shirt off his back if needed.

In SAC, we were assigned to fly in "hard" crews. Unless you had an illness, were on military leave, or were in individual ground training, you would always fly and sit on alert with the same crew members. This proved to be a critical factor for us because it quickly became apparent with subsequent flights that our new commander was more than a little rusty from his time on campus. I had suddenly gone from a low-time copilot being mentored by an IP to an aircraft commander in the right seat. I was put in a tough spot because the ultimate authority for the aircraft rested with him, but if things weren't said or done, sometimes very quickly, we would all die. It seemed with around half the sorties we flew, there would be some kind of challenge to deal with, sometimes as simple as turning left rather than right or a needed reminder we should consider descending soon. Other times, it was worse, even hair-raising.

It turns out that I was a good match for him when it came to air sense and getting back on the ground safely. I tried to support him in an affable manner without overstepping my authority. Yet there were times when direct intervention was necessary. Occasionally, there would be other copilots substituting for me. Afterward, they sometimes pulled me aside to discuss their flight with the crew. Even substitute navigators or boom operators would, every now and then, walk away after a flight unsettled by the events that occurred during the mission.

As time went on, his skill in the aircraft didn't improve much. He was just one of those individuals who really didn't belong in the cockpit, and through an unlikely sequence of events, found himself in charge of one. I felt boxed in because the head of training (the one who requalified him) flew with him at a previous assignment. Going to the OPS officer (operations officer) to discuss this matter would be pointless because he was already informed through both the head of training and quiet discussions with other squadron members. Trying to sideline this individual in a desk job while getting the Management Personnel Center to find a replacement would cause the Air Force to lose another twelve or so pilots to the civilian world. In the meantime, the squadron would struggle to stay mission-ready on limited personnel. Lastly, and most importantly, no first lieutenant relishes the prospect of talking to his OPS officer in a private conversation in his office with the door closed about an aircraft commander he personally feels needs a new job title. It would not be a comfortable conversation to have and probably wouldn't end well for the first lieutenant. Still, I felt I needed a break. My hair was already turning gray without this kind of help, so I tried a different approach. One day, I met with the OPS officer in his office and asked to be reassigned to the standards and evaluation section as a copilot. This pseudo-promotion would get me off the crew and perhaps slow the pace of my graying hair, but he never got back to me on that request. So, I had my answer as to how things stood with our crew when we flew. Although I wasn't really in charge of the flight, I was the one responsible for the safe outcome of the flight.

By this time, I was heavily involved with flying the T-38. If the crew were scheduled for a short flight in the KC-135 or even just a pattern-ride in the tanker to do approaches and landings, I would fly the T-38 before and after the KC-135 flight and transition between these two very different aircraft seamlessly. This had the effect of greatly sharpening my skills and focus in both aircraft and helped with my confidence too. It also had the added benefit of being fun.

An exciting routine in my monthly schedule had also developed. Bob Aboe, another single guy, and I were scheduled on the same alert cycle as copilots. Almost without exception, once we finished our seven-day tour on alert, we would leave the alert facility and drive directly to the T-38 hangar. As soon as we could file a flight plan, pack, then preflight the aircraft, and start the engines, we would be gone for three-and-a-half days. We flew all over the country, logging hundreds of hours together over the course of a couple of years.

Flying with Aboe was an adventure in itself. He was a short, stumpy Italian whose vertically challenged frame couldn't possibly contain all the charisma within it. That charisma found its outlet in charming women all over the country and thinking of new ways to get around, if not breaking, the few regulations that were imposed on our T-38 flying. He was born into a military family. His father was an Army colonel. But Bob was born to be a fighter pilot. He went through AFROTC in college, earned his UPT slot, graduated either first or second in his pilot training class, and was absolutely crushed on assignment night when he found out he was assigned a tanker to Grand Forks, North Dakota, rather than a fighter aircraft somewhere warmer. The T-38 flying was a poor substitute for him. Nevertheless, he approached it with the same innate aggressiveness he would have displayed in an F-15 fighter. A lot of times, I was there to hold him back as best I could. He, in turn, helped me overcome my own overly cautious outlook on flying and challenged me to get better. Of course, I didn't completely abandon those conservative instincts. I did draw the line at not flying under a bridge with him. Despite his persistent attempts to change my mind, I said no and probably saved both our flying careers with that choice. Fortunately, we were never called on the carpet for our many other transgressions. Some of our explanations of events would have lacked credibility. But I always treasured our time together in that aircraft and the wonderful friendship that developed.

As I have mentioned before, the primary job of a KC-135 and its crew was to sit on alert, awaiting a nuclear attack on the country. If an attack came and the alarm sounded, overburdened with fuel the tanker would stagger into the air, head north, and at a certain point, offload every ounce of fuel it could to a B-52 bomber. Then it would try to land at a designated field before it flamed out in the air.

But it was also capable of air refueling just about every fixed-wing aircraft in the US military, which made it a valuable resource for exercises and deployments. Our squadron would routinely be tasked, on a limited basis, to support this flying in Europe, Asia, Alaska, and the Middle East. These were coveted assignments for tanker crews because you would leave the base for forty-five days or so and do something different, like drag some fighters across the Atlantic or air refuel a massive C-5 carrying Marines and their equipment to the Middle East. You would also end up with about the same amount of flying time in those forty-five days as you would in ten months just doing your regular flying at Grand Forks. For tanker copilots looking to upgrade to the left seat, you needed to be deployed on as many of these forty-five-day trips as possible to reach the minimum amount of flying time required by SAC to upgrade.

I mention all this because tanker crew schedulers would try to distribute these trips equitably, with every crew getting their chance to deploy somewhere to gain experience and build time while supporting other military missions and exercises. Our crew, however, was quietly being pushed down the list due to our "experience level." We were eventually given the nod to go and were sent over to Royal Air Force (RAF) Fairford in England, an old WWII bomber base upgraded to support our needs, about seventy-five miles west of London. We left at three o'clock in the afternoon from Grand Forks, flew across the Atlantic at night, and arrived at our destination as the sun rose over that historic island. It was quite a sight to see, especially after flying all night. Now we just needed some rest and to find out our flying schedule for the rest of the deployment.

We had about four days to adjust ourselves to the time zone change, and then we were up again, this time in a formation of tankers orbiting to refuel fighters involved in an exercise. The exercise was to continue the following day, but it was canceled due to the weather.

So, the next time we found ourselves in the air, we were on our way to Saudi Arabia to join a tanker task force in Riyadh, their capital. Our job would be to provide air-refueling support for the E-3A Airborne Warning and Control System (AWACS) aircraft, a flying radar station that served as an early warning and defensive system that operated twenty-four hours a day. It was both remarkable and enjoyable to leave Grand Forks, North Dakota, ending up a day later in England and a few days after that in Saudi Arabia. Each was strikingly different from the other two with both its climate and its history. A more immediate concern for me, however, was getting sunblock in Riyadh, even though it was November. I certainly didn't pack that in Grand Forks. They didn't even sell that back in Grand Forks.

This time we had a few days of rest in Riyadh, then we were back on a crew bus to go fly a refueling mission. Our first flight there was scheduled with an Air Force captain who would ride with us to basically show us the ropes of the operation. He gave us a briefing in the single-wide trailer that served as Base Operations and then took us out to the airplane already serviced and fueled. As fortune would have it, the captain was a furloughed American Airlines pilot who came back into the

Air Force to keep a roof over his head and was waiting to be recalled by American Airlines. His punishment for disloyalty to the Air Force for initially leaving was to be assigned to Riyadh to fill this position, but he handled it well.

That could not be said for our aircraft commander that day. He chose to fly the leg, and on climb-out, he let his airspeed get too high. I made some comments about it, but it didn't register with him until I said we were going to overspeed the airplane as we approached 350 knots. He responded by commanding the autopilot to pull the nose up aggressively and then left it up as the airspeed bled off. As he approached 250 knots, I had to remind him to shallow out the climb so he could regain proper climb speed, which he did.

We made it to the refueling area and the rendezvous point with the AWACS aircraft and successfully accomplished the mission, but inside the aircraft, things didn't go smoothly. We just didn't seem to be working well as a crew that day. Coming back to the base, despite my gentle reminders and prodding, we descended way too early and ended up being level at five thousand feet while fifty miles from the field. Normally you would plan on being thirty miles out at ten thousand feet. That was a lot of wasted fuel, but it also reflected badly on us as a crew and our squadron. I kept my decorum, but I was quietly upset about the whole sortie.

We landed, taxied in, shut down the engines, and headed back to the trailer after the checklists were completed to debrief. The ride-along captain just touched on a few mission-specific items with us that would help us deal with upcoming flights and signed us off as mission-ready.

So, we were "good to go" on paper. I headed out the trailer door to check on the crew bus as the ride-along captain was exiting too. As soon as the door closed and we were outside in the bright sunshine of Saudi Arabia, he began to speak in a matter-of-fact tone. He said he was very impressed with my performance as copilot, and both the navigator and the boom operator were excellent at their jobs. Then he said if I didn't keep a close eye on the aircraft commander, he was going to kill us. At this point, it was obvious to me he wanted to get me alone to deliver his message, but it wasn't necessary. I had been dealing with the issue for some time now. One of the reasons we had been held back from deploying from Grand Forks for so long, I felt, was the squadron leadership wanted to be certain I could deal with it. Now the word of how we were doing was most likely going to filter back to Grand Forks. But I thanked the captain for his concern and assured him this was something I was accustomed to doing. Then I promised myself I would try harder to take care of it, for everyone's sake.

We managed to stay out of trouble for the rest of the deployment, both in Saudi Arabia and England, but it took some effort. Soon enough, our forty-five days were up, and we flew back to North Dakota. By now, it was January, and we were dreading the thought of trying to start our cars in the sub-zero temperatures we were expecting. So, after landing around eleven o'clock in the evening, and before we began filling out the paperwork from our flight and the deployment, we plugged in the engine block heaters of our vehicles. By the time we were through with the paperwork, the cars were more than ready to start. And we were more than ready to be home. We had survived the forty-five days, and I felt a sense of relief. We were all back and in one piece. I could relax a bit.

After a long deployment like ours, you were allowed a few days off to get resettled and reacclimated. Aboe left a message in my squadron box saying we had a T-38 reserved in the morning for a weekend cross country, which was the perfect way for me to resettle and reacclimate. So, after a short night's sleep in the apartment, off we went to find some warm sunshine, which he needed more than I. As I reminded him, I was just in Saudi Arabia. We returned on Sunday to Grand Forks, and all too soon, we found ourselves back on our seven-day alert cycle followed by a three-and-a-half-day stretch of T-38 cross-country flying. Like being required to eat all your vegetables before getting dessert, alert was not fun, but knowing the T-38 was waiting for us after we were released made the time almost palatable to swallow, unlike the vegetables they fed us in the dining hall. So, we waited for our Thursday morning release time. We had spent the week faithfully eating our "vegetables," and now it was time for "dessert." We raced over to the T-38 hangar, more than just eager to leave the base. We had to be back by Sunday. Until then, we were free. And we had a T-38 at our disposal.

Words can't express how intoxicating this freedom could be. And Bob was the perfect partner to share this freedom with. I have never laughed so hard, especially wearing an oxygen mask, or had so much fun in an airplane as we talked and flew about the country. The T-38 has no autopilot, so holding altitude could be a problem when we began to laugh. But it was a wonderful problem to manage. And there was no better release from the stressful tanker flying than being in a T-38 at thirty-nine thousand feet on a clear, sunny day.

We were back on the squadron scheduling board to fly a local mission now, so we mission-planned on a Tuesday following our release from alert. I relayed my suspicions to the crew that a no-notice check ride was a likelihood because the standards and evaluation check airmen were fond of doing this to crews just back from deployment. I didn't mention my conversation with the ride-along captain in Saudi Arabia and how I assumed he made a phone call.

Sure enough, the evaluators were there to greet us as we checked in for the flight the following morning. Unfortunately, things didn't go well for our crew on that day. Procedures specified in the manuals sometimes are abbreviated by crews when they are deployed, and checklist discipline can become lax. And SAC had a lot of procedures and checklists. Both the navigator and the boom operator failed because of noncompliance with some of those procedures. When we got back to the traffic pattern in Grand Forks, I did my approaches and landings without any issues. After a multiple-seat swap, our aircraft commander did his approaches and landing. It was a blustery day with some good crosswinds, and he didn't correct for it adequately. The evaluator ended up momentarily taking the airplane away from him. We made a full stop, parked the airplane, and debriefed back at the squadron. As it turned out, everyone failed except me. This flight also began the process of removing the aircraft commander from a regular crew position to more of a desk job. It didn't happen overnight because they needed to find a replacement, but the wheels did start turning to find him a new position. I assumed they felt they could no longer ignore the problem. As for me, I had no way of finding out if the ride-along captain in Saudi Arabia got word back to Grand Forks that they had a problem with the left seat position of our crew. But if that was the case, he did everyone a favor, including the aircraft commander. And with a twist of irony worthy of an O. Henry story, he was promoted to the position of Squadron Flight Safety Officer.

CHAPTER 9
Reckless Abandonment

I have gone into a fair amount of detail about squadron life in North Dakota to help explain my rediscovery of personal faith. You could be forgiven for thinking, "Oh, let me guess. He discovers God again because he feels the hand of the Almighty extricating him from the many dangers he experiences in the cockpit of the KC-135. Like the cliché states, 'No atheists in the foxholes,' only this foxhole is an airborne version. It sounds like the standard fare served up on a Sunday morning televangelist program." It's a bit darker. My experience actually drove me in the opposite direction.

As soon as I realized the new aircraft commander was a threat to life and limb, I began to up my game. I studied more, became more familiar with regulations, emergency checklists, and procedures, and thought through scenarios I might encounter. But at some point, I had to admit to myself that death was a possibility since I couldn't control everything. It was depressing at first because I felt trapped. Though unspoken, the squadron knew the situation and decided, in the name of mission-readiness, to turn a blind eye. This had the effect of dumping the problem on an inexperienced copilot, namely me. Had I at least been given the courtesy of an informal acknowledgment of the situation by either the OPS officer, the Chief of Training, or even a tanker IP in our flight, it would have had a much more positive effect on my attitude. For whatever reason, no one chose to do so, leaving me to feel like I was marooned on an island with no rescue in sight. Besides the depressing aspects of this situation, most normal people would feel some anger and resentment, and I was no different.

Yet, you cannot live your life that way for long without pernicious effects, and I honestly felt my time would soon come to an end anyway. So, I changed my attitude. Rather than dwell on the morbid, I would live my life one day at a time. If death came the next day, at least I felt like I would go down swinging for the fences rather than a called strike. This had a liberating effect on my dark outlook toward life. I can recall one time when Aboe and I were out in the local area assigned by Air Traffic Control for T-38s to go play. I was in the front seat with the nose of the aircraft pointed down at a steep angle, throttles set at full power, picking up airspeed while looking for 450–500 knots to start a loop. I thought to myself, "I may be dead tomorrow but I'm definitely not dead today!" The g-meter on the cockpit panel swung upwards to about four and a half as I pulled back on the stick, and the North Dakota landscape soon filled the top of the canopy. I relaxed a bit of stick pressure at the top only to pull back hard again as we came out of the bottom of our loop, those g-forces making an encore appearance. Sometimes life can be good. Really good.

So, my time in the T-38 became an escape from my tanker problem, and I tried escaping every chance I could. Mostly it was cross-country flying, but at my persistent request, a few of us were requalified to fly formation by the local T-38 IPs. It was twice the fun as single-ship flights, so we tried to fly it as much as we could and subsequently got to be pretty good at it. We also did low-level flights, sometimes on military tracks designed for it, sometimes not.

But as wonderful as all those times flying in a T-38 were, I really wasn't escaping. This would cause me to become morose, often at times when I was alone. I could tell myself to live my life one day at a time, but it was another thing for me to do successfully each and every day. I just wasn't built that way. I was a freshman in high school when I found myself in that empty classroom, trying to map out my future at age fifteen. I was an FAA instrument-rated pilot before I even started UPT so I could increase my chances of success in the program. I even bought life insurance when I was eighteen because I had read pilots had a difficult time getting coverage. I must have been that agent's youngest client ever to purchase a whole-life policy.

Temperamentally, I was a long-term planner to my core. So, for me to accede to a "here-today-gone-tomorrow" outlook took a lot of effort. Some days were better than others. Yet I couldn't see any other way of dealing with the issue with my completely secular outlook on life. Yes, life is tentative. It could easily end in a big ball of flames for me despite my best efforts.

And you wouldn't know it. This was vividly illustrated to me one afternoon while I was on alert, and we had an alert exercise occur. During such exercises, the klaxon sounds all over the base and the alert facility warning of a possible attack. The alert crews must quickly race to their aircraft and start their engines while simultaneously decoding a secure radio broadcast message to see if it was merely an exercise or if it was the real thing. If it was real, we would launch. Otherwise, we might end up taxiing the aircraft down the runway to simulate taking off or remain parked in position. We would do whatever was called for in the decoded message. In this case, we were to remain in position. What made this alert exercise a national event was the B-52 parked almost directly across the ramp from our aircraft caught fire. A fuel line feeding directly into the combustion section of the starting engine ruptured, in short, producing an uncontained fire. The crew evacuated the aircraft when warned over the radio about this unexpected blaze enveloping the engine pod and threatening to move to their right wing. But in their haste to exit the aircraft, the pilots shut off the aircraft battery before pulling the engine fire handle. This had the effect of keeping the engine fuel shut-off valve open and fuel continuously hemorrhaging into the combustion section and surrounding areas.

Flames shot high into the sky, and chaos ensued as our crew watched from our front-row seats across the ramp. It was a frantic scene with fire trucks scrambling, their lights flashing and horns blaring, the security police trying to establish a perimeter around the aircraft, the aircraft crew trying not to become roadkill, while excited voices filled the radio frequency as the bomber continued to burn. Eventually, we taxied all the functioning aircraft down to the opposite side of the field. We left the engines running in case we had to launch for emergency relocation.

After almost three hours, the fire was extinguished by a couple of brave firefighters who ran into the burning B-52, turned on the battery, pushed in the engine fire handle to its normal position, then reengaged it by pulling it to close the fuel shut-off valve. That worked to everyone's relief. The next day the story made front-page news in papers across the country. Walter Cronkite included it in his nightly broadcast for CBS News, and our wing commander was replaced a short while later. The B-52 survived to fly again, and the aircraft commander eventually became a standards-and-evaluation pilot in the bomber squadron.

Yet even though it was widely reported, the stories themselves only gave cursory coverage of this event. Had any of those journalists probed deeper, they would have discovered some disturbing facts to add to their original reports. For one, not only was a fully fueled B-52 with an uncontained fire a huge explosive risk, but there were nuclear weapons on board. Those nuclear weapons were not capable of detonating, but the heat from the fire could cause the conventional explosives in the weapons to detonate, rupturing the casings and releasing the radioactive material. There was a very stiff eastward wind that day that could have carried the plutonium particles released from the explosion toward the town of Grand Forks, twelve miles east and beyond. We would have been facing our version of Chernobyl in the upper Midwest.

There would have been horrendous consequences from this that would be felt for generations.

We were all fortunate that night to achieve the outcome we did. Just one or two more wrong moves or bad breaks and the history books would not be telling a kind story about us. Naturally, I gave the incident a lot of thought afterward. Among other things, I asked, "Had I perished that day, what then?" Since my college days, the answer was, well, nothing because death was the end of existence. At this point, things were changing to allow for a different answer to that question. The answer wasn't there yet, but at least it was on the horizon. And after this incident, I am profoundly grateful to have seen it arrive.

CHAPTER 10
"Play Ball!"

Several months earlier, I was back in Omaha on leave. My father had suffered a heart attack and had undergone triple bypass surgery a month prior to this. Considering his condition, I thought it would be prudent to spend my leave time at home. It was enjoyable being back in Omaha, spending time with my parents, visiting with my old high school friends, and not having to worry about a flight schedule. It was Memorial Day, 1980. Tom Rossi called the house saying there was going to be a pickup softball game at a field near the Mutual of Omaha headquarters building and invited me to play. Now I hadn't played softball in years, and I was hesitant. Other than Tom, I wouldn't know anyone there, and my meager softball skills probably hadn't improved. I didn't want to embarrass myself in front of a bunch of strangers, and I told him as much. He said not to worry about it. It wasn't that kind of game or crowd, and to pick up Donahue, another high school friend, on the way. "Well, if Denny is coming, I probably won't be the worst player there," I thought, laughing to myself. Still, I said I would think about it.

I hung up the phone and was weighing whether to go when I once again heard the quiet voice. It said, "Go ahead and play. You will meet the woman you are going to marry." Wow. Talk about coming from out of left field! "I must be truly losing my mind," I thought. I certainly didn't need or want this kind of distraction in my life. I wanted to stay focused on building flying time so I could exit the Air Force and fly for a major carrier. That was the plan. That was what the quiet voice had been all about since I first heard it. "Be an airline pilot." Where did this come from all of the sudden? "A wife, really?" I thought. Having to support a wife and a family might actually force me to stay in the Air Force and keep me from my chosen career field! "This doesn't make any sense!"

Now I was facing another dilemma. I could try to forget about my matchmaking revelation from beyond and tell Rossi I wasn't going to play. But the issue of this latest voice experience and my sanity would remain unsettled. So, I decided to pick up Denny and go to the game, hoping not to embarrass myself too much on the field and see what would happen.

You both know the story well. Rossi arrived at the softball field ahead of us, so he mentioned to this group of holiday softball players that he invited two of his high school classmates to join in the fun. Someone asked what we were like, and Tom, using his sharp mind honed with law-school training, replied with a checklist of my best attributes, saying, "Well, one of them is an officer in the Air Force. He flies jets, drives a Camaro, and lifts weights." At which point, your mother, showing her innate good sense, intelligence, and judgment of character, said, "Tell us about the other one."

As for the game, neither your mother nor I embarrassed ourselves too much on the field. Even Denny did well. Tom was right about it not being the kind of hypercompetitive group that would focus on winning at the expense of enjoying the afternoon. At the Memorial Day party after the game, your mother approached me because I was the only guy there not drinking alcohol, instead drinking orange juice I had purchased on the way to the party. She was intrigued by that and asked if I was willing to share. As the party was breaking up at the end of the evening, she asked me to join a small group who were going to the horse racing track later in the week. I guess she was trying to figure out if this quiet teetotaler had any vices at this point. At the track, it turns out she did a better job of picking winners than I did. On the track, at least, because I was definitely smitten with her by then.

My leave time was expiring soon, so I had to leave Omaha and return to North Dakota, but your mother and I continued to see each other. The T-38 proved very helpful in this process so our relationship could flourish. But if it hadn't been for the quiet voice, it might not have ever happened. The voice proved to be 6-for-6 in its guidance and predictions. Much better than either Denise or I at the track. Despite all its success, however, I was unwilling to seriously examine its origins. Just like each previous occurrence, that examination would have to wait for another day.

The serious reflection I was putting off allowed me to focus like a laser on building flying time for a post–Air Force career while avoiding some hard questions about faith. Still, if I were to be honest, I wasn't completely successful in avoiding those questions. There were a few occasions when I allowed myself to confront the issue. After all, any superficial review of my past would scream of either astonishingly good fortune or a divine influence. As a fifteen-year-old, I "chose" an incredibly difficult profession to enter after ten minutes worth of consideration. It was a career field I knew next to nothing about, and the first step on my way required me to pass all the physical, mental, and psychological exams administered by the Air Force. This was by no means easy. Most applicants didn't make it beyond this point, but I was one of the fortunate few. Another fortunate choice was enrolling in perhaps the only university AFROTC program that could secure a UPT slot for me after my less-than-impressive performance at AFROTC summer camp. You may recall I had some exceptional help with my choice of post-secondary education back in high school. I also had some help in deciding to do a full-court press to improve my grades in my sophomore year of college. If I hadn't, I would not have even been selected as an alternate for UPT. Against my better judgment, I gambled I would be given a slot as an alternate for pilot training after my conference with Col. Hyde my junior year at CSU. The consensus among the staff was I would leave the AFROTC program, so they were surprised to learn I had signed the intent-to-commission letter. If they had learned my reasoning behind it, they would have quickly shredded the document I signed and pointed me toward the door. And I wouldn't blame them for doing it. In pilot training, I was informed I was going to fly a tanker way up north somewhere, and I found myself flying a KC-135 stationed in Grand Forks, about as far north as you could get without being Canadian.

But this last voice experience was either the capstone of craziness for me or a divine signpost for faith. That's because I presently found myself seriously involved with a woman I was informed I would meet at the softball game and later marry. It was almost a miracle I was even in town that weekend to participate in the game rather than out logging hours in the T-38. Yet, it happened. All of it happened. And I knew I needed to address the issues that resulted from these encounters. During each of those rare instances where I found myself confronting those issues, I would walk right up to that line of faith I needed to cross, turn around, and walk back.

The simple answer to this was I knew, in my heart of hearts, what was happening to me and where it was coming from. I also knew what was required from me if I crossed that line, and I wasn't ready. Surrendering to His will wasn't going to fly in my skies, even though I seemed to be assiduously following the flight plan He had filed for me. Better to focus on collecting flight hours and increasing my aeronautical skills for my post–Air Force career, rather than dealing with hard choices of faith. For now, it would be my will rather than His, and all the cognitive dissonance it produced would be dealt with at another time.

CHAPTER 11
Sheppard Air Force Base

It was the last weekend in May of 1981, and Aboe and I were in the Base Operations building at Offutt AFB. We had left Grand Forks earlier that morning on the first leg of our weekend cross-country in the T-38. North Dakota routinely clings to its winter season. Even though it was almost June, you could still find isolated patches of snow on the ground in areas of continuous shade, and furnaces could still be needed during the night. When we arrived in Omaha, we found ourselves overdressed for the warm weather we were experiencing as we popped open the canopies of the aircraft. We would have to shed the flight jackets we wore for the next leg of our trip.

We were using Offutt as a fuel stop on our way to Reese AFB. Reese provided all the aircraft and necessary support for the T-38 Detachment in Grand Forks. Almost two years earlier,

Reese also provided me, which I had mixed feelings about, but the assignment was growing on me. Staying comfortable and current flying in the KC-135 always proved difficult due to our lack of scheduled flying time, and I spent half of each month waking up in the alert facility rather than my apartment. Fortunately, fate provided me with a twin-engine, supersonic coping mechanism that helped compensate for these hardships. On days like today, I felt that fate was more than making up for the hardships I experienced.

We were flying to Reese because Joel asked us to swap out the T-38 we were flying for a new member of his small fleet. It would be waiting for us once we landed. We needed to make a quick refueling stop because the weather forecast called for thunderstorms later in the day in Lubbock.

Offutt could pose a problem as a refueling stop because it wasn't first-come-first-served when it came to topping off our tanks. Priority was given to general and flag-ranked officers and their aircraft. Since Offutt was the headquarters of the Strategic Air Command, it had a lot of generals, and occasionally some admirals, coming and going. You could be stuck at the bottom of the refueling list for a while on bad "general" days. Bob and I found a way around this problem that often worked. The aircraft refuelers and the crew chiefs for aircraft transiting Offutt were not military members. They were civilians hired by the refueling contractor for the base. By actually being friendly with them, getting to know their names, and talking with them during aircraft walkarounds, we would oftentimes get moved to the top of the refueling list. I guess the generals, the admirals, and their staff were too preoccupied to figure this out as they waited while we were being serviced.

What really sealed the deal on service for us was our willingness to reciprocate their generosity toward us and our jet. They liked high-performance aircraft, so one day, they asked if we could do a high-speed flyby after we took off. We had the fuel for it, so we said sure; just give us a couple of minutes after we get the gear up.

They scrambled into their service vehicle as soon as they unplugged the air cart from our aircraft and pulled the chocks. They wanted to be near the runway for a better view when we came back around. Bob was in the front seat that morning. So, as we were taxiing toward the runway, he requested the control tower to amend our clearance to include the flyby. We were given the clearance we requested, and our altitude restriction was lifted from four thousand feet to ten thousand feet. We departed on runway 13, pulled up into the visual traffic pattern, and instead of dropping the gear and flaps on downwind to prepare for a landing, Bob rolled off the perch clean and fast. The force of gravity came into play, helping our airspeed quickly reach the FAA maximum allowable of three hundred knots for the T-38 below ten thousand feet. Bob stopped our descent about ten feet above the runway, and by this time, we MAY have been traveling at more than three hundred knots. It's hard to say for certain, but if so, it wasn't for long because we quickly reached the opposite end of the runway, and now we needed to climb. Bob pulled back on the stick, the g-meter on the instrument panel registering almost five Gs, and the aircraft responded by rocketing straight up. The vertical velocity indicator (VVI) was pegged at plus-six thousand feet a minute, and in no time at all, we reached our ten-thousand-feet restriction. Aboe did show some restraint. At least he didn't reengage the afterburners, but it was still a loud and gaudy spectacle by a couple of SAC's most disgruntled copilots at the headquarters of the most staid, restrictive command in the Air Force. The crew chiefs loved it. We heard about it the next time we came through, and we were lucky it was only from them that we heard about it. Those higher up in the command structure almost certainly would have found it objectionable had they been a witness. I'm sure if they weren't exactly a witness, many of them would have heard it. But as far as we were concerned, our departure from Offutt was nothing more than returning a favor to some friends. And we would return their favors many more times in a similar fashion before we left the T-38 for the left seat of the tanker. I guess somebody must have really been looking out for us back then.

There would be no flyby today, though. We were trying to get to Reese before a thunderstorm engulfed the Texas panhandle, so we were counting on our friends to get us in and out quickly. They didn't disappoint, telling us we were next in line for fuel as we headed for the entrance to Base Ops. I asked Bob to check on the weather forecast while I made a quick phone call to Denise at her workplace. Back then, there were no cell phones, and any phone call outside your area code included additional charges. I just wanted to take advantage of our stop in Omaha to say a quick hello. I finished up the phone call and sought out Bob in the flight crew planning room. It looked like the fuelers were through, so I asked Bob about the weather forecast, and he said it still looked good for our arrival time. We then headed out the door for our aircraft parked just a short walk across the ramp.

Bob was in the front cockpit today, and I was in the rear one. Tomorrow we would swap. It didn't make much difference which seat we occupied. We shared almost everything, including the landings. Backseat landings by copilots were strictly forbidden by regulations. No training was provided for it during our T-38 requalification program, so no backseat landings were allowed. Our group of copilots quietly instituted a T-38 requalification program that took care of this thoughtless oversight by the program's creators. I landed from the backseat of the T-38 on my very first flight with Aboe in the front seat and hadn't stopped since. By this time, we each had more backseat landings than all but the most seasoned T-38 IPs in Air Training Command. We just had to be sure the aircraft logbook reflected all landings were assigned to the front seater. We wouldn't want anyone to think we were a couple of scofflaws.

We weren't thinking about any of this, of course. We needed to get airborne in case the thunderstorm made an early appearance over our West Texas destination, so we walked briskly to the aircraft. Bob strapped into the front cockpit while I did the walkaround. Soon enough, I was strapping into the rear seat, performing checklist items, and copying the clearance as it was read to us over the radio. We took care of a few more checklist items, and after the air cart was up and running, Bob started the engines. He then gave the signal to disconnect the air cart, and while the crew chief was occupied with that chore, we continued running the checklist down to the flight control check. Bob waited until the crew chief was once again in front of our aircraft so he could get confirmation of correct positioning, with the crew chief using hand signals as Bob moved the flight controls. We then held up our ejection seat and canopy safety pins to signal those systems were now capable of being armed for use or activated. The crew chief gave us a thumbs up, so we stowed them in their retainer boxes. Aboe then gave the hand signal for the chocks to be pulled. This was all performed in a rapid, yet controlled pace, with us responding to the checklist items called for over the intercom system between cockpits while using hand signals with the crew chief. It was by now quite routine for us, but it was an important, disciplined approach to getting both us and the aircraft ready for departure. It could be done quickly but not carelessly.

We received taxi clearance to the departure end of runway 31, so we taxied with our canopies open and our jackets off, enjoying the wonderful mid-morning weather on our nearly two-mile trip to the far end of the field. As we approached the runway threshold, we lowered the canopies, took care of a few more checklist items, then switched over to tower frequency. After checking in with them, we were cleared onto runway 31 to hold.

With the canopies closed, the cockpits were now pressurized and much quieter. We both had our green helmet visors down to protect against the bright sunlight, and we were able to hear our relaxed breathing over the hot mic connections wired into our oxygen masks and helmets.

The high-pitched hum of the twin J85-GE 5 Series engines provided background noise as they idled on the runway. Tower was checking with departure control to see if the airspace was clear before we launched into it. After a minute, the tower called to give us the wind direction and speed, then directed us to fly runway heading, climb and maintain four thousand feet, and cleared us for takeoff. Aboe repeated back the clearance, and the gentle, reassuring hum of those idling engines was about to change. He pushed up the throttles from idle to full power while practically standing on the brake pedals to keep the jet locked in position. The engines responded with a loud, high-frequency shrill while we both made a quick check of the engine gauges to confirm normal takeoff readings. The small brakes on the small wheels strained mightily to hold the aircraft in position while the aircraft shook, trying to break free from the constraints they were providing. The gauge readings looked good, so Bob released the brakes while simultaneously pushing the throttles forward over the detent in the throttle quadrant to engage the afterburners. And now it got REALLY LOUD as the throttles went all the way to the stops. The high-pitched shrill dropped in tone to settle into a deeper, more overpowering, thunderous roar. The fuel flow gauges leaped to their max readings as huge amounts of fuel were being force-fed into the engine's afterburner section. Instantly it was transformed from a liquid state into an explosive gas. The nozzle actuators in the tailpipes, those variable apertures regulating thrust exiting the engine, snapped open to their maximum limits to accommodate for this sudden increase in power coming from the afterburners.

We both felt a noticeable shove backwards into our seats as this rapid increase in thrust pushed the aircraft forward while rendering our ears incapable of hearing anything but the sounds of those engines. Yet, even with the afterburners fully engaged and the brakes released, the aircraft initially just crept forward. The T-38 weighs almost six tons fully fueled. Each engine produced up to 2,900 pounds of thrust in afterburner mode. It would take a second to get those tires really moving forward, but once they started rolling, the aircraft gained momentum quickly. Fifteen to twenty seconds later, you would be at 135 knots, pulling back slightly on the stick to bring the nose gear off the runway and establishing the takeoff attitude. Shortly after that, it would reach 160 knots and fly off the runway on its own, but not before gravity made its last, desperate attempt to reclaim it. TAP, TAP, TAP, TAP, TAP. The T-38 has small, thin wings. For such a handicapped creature to achieve the lift necessary to break free from the Earth's pull, it needed powerful engines and a lot of speed. To achieve that speed, you needed a long runway, a minimum of eight thousand feet. Those taps came from getting close to the liftoff speed, one wing at a time. One wing would achieve liftoff, but not quite so for the other. So, the first wing would settle back onto the support of its gear, waiting for its mate to catch up. Now the other wing was ready to fly, and it would rise. This time the first wing wasn't quite ready to catch up to it, so the process would repeat itself—five quick taps worth. That was enough to get both wings ready to rise together and vanquish the Earth's claim on the aircraft.

In the cockpit, you would know when the struggle with gravity was over by both your VVI and altimeter readings showing climb indications. The landing gear would then be retracted, followed shortly thereafter by the flaps. It had to be done in a brisk fashion, or you would risk exceeding the operational speed limits for both the gear and flaps as you accelerated forward. The afterburners came last, retarding the throttles just past the detent to settle back into the full-power setting. The noise level was reduced with this last action but not by much. It would only reach more tolerable levels once you reached the climb speed of three hundred knots. By this time, much of the noise seemed to get caught up in the jet's slipstream and disappear behind us, too slow to keep up as the engines propelled us forward.

We soon switched over from departure control to Minneapolis Center and were climbing, passing ten thousand feet on our way to thirty-nine thousand feet while heading southwest. We leveled off ten minutes later with smooth air and clear skies

Sheppard Air Force Base

over Nebraska and Kansas, but toward Oklahoma, the sky was clouding over. As we sped closer to Reese, we were dodging cloud buildups. At around 150 miles northeast of the base, I contacted Reese's weather reporting facility, known as Metro, to get an update on their weather. It turned out both the weather briefings for our destination were slightly incorrect. Reese was currently closed due to a thunderstorm overhead. The storm we were trying to beat formed faster than forecasted.

Now we had some decisions to make.

Unlike the tanker, which could loiter all day, depending on the amount of fuel it carried, the T-38 was limited. If your destination was temporarily closed, you needed a quick alternate plan because ninety-nine times out of one hundred, you weren't holding until the field reopened. This was our situation. A quick check of alternatives yielded two choices, neither of them very good. One was Cannon AFB, one hundred miles north of Reese in New Mexico, but the weather was threatening to strike there. The other was Sheppard AFB, located in North Texas. The weather system was just clearing there. We would have to fight our way through the system to reach it, but once we did, we could land. Rather than risk being too late again, we chose Sheppard.

We were already cruising at thirty-nine thousand feet, but we were in the clouds, and it was turbulent. Hoping to get out of the turbulence and save on fuel for our new destination, we requested a higher altitude as we turned eastward toward Sheppard. If we were lucky, we might even break out on top, so we wouldn't need radar vectors from ATC to avoid the storm cells. We eventually reached forty-seven thousand feet. We requested forty-nine thousand feet, but due to the atmospheric conditions, we were barely holding forty-seven thousand. And we were still getting tossed around in the clouds. This wasn't surprising. Thunderstorms in Texas can sometimes reach halfway to the moon, and today seemed to be one of those days.

This was also unfortunate. We were flying blind when it came to encountering storm cells embedded in the clouds. Those cells, with their lightning, turbulence, and possible hail, have occasionally proven powerful enough to bring down military jets and commercial airliners. The hail alone, if large enough, is capable of cracking the cockpit windows, injuring the wings, and wreaking havoc on the aircraft's engines. The T-38 was a wonderfully designed jet, but it wasn't equipped with weather radar. We would be entirely dependent on ATC to steer us clear of any storm cells in our path. And we had to hope we didn't lose our one comm radio with its emergency backup as we tried to avoid them.

As if we didn't have enough to deal with, there was one more problem that required our attention. Since we leveled off at forty-seven thousand feet, and despite using full-power settings with the throttles, we found ourselves slowly losing our airspeed. The Mach-speed-indicator needle was steadily inching backward to the point where it would soon be hidden from view. It didn't help matters that we had turned on the engine anti-icing system to prevent the engine inlet guide vanes and the bullet nose in the engine air inlet duct from icing up and disrupting airflow. It worked by heating up those components with hot, compressed air siphoned off the engine. The tradeoff was less thrust coming out of the tailpipes. Unfortunately, we didn't have any choice in the matter. We were still in the clouds and subject to icing. In a nutshell, this meant our engines were slowly being starved of air. Eventually, they would let us know when it reached the critical point by compressor stalling, sounding like your grandfather's backfiring old Pontiac, then perhaps flaming out. At this point, we would have no choice but to descend.

To sum up our situation, we couldn't climb higher so we might see and avoid the storm cells. We didn't want to go any lower because of the roiling, agitated air mass and other unseen dangers that were lurking beneath us. And it was only a matter of time before we could no longer maintain our present altitude and be forced to descend. In the interim, we were flying blind and trusting ATC to look out for our best interests when it came to avoiding the kinds of storm cells presently over Reese. This was not an enviable situation to be in. Nevertheless, there we were.

It turns out we made the right decision, and fortune began to smile on us during all this turmoil. We were just too preoccupied by our circumstances to realize it. Cannon AFB got clobbered by the storm system soon after we turned eastward toward Sheppard. ATC had done a wonderful job steering us around the weather, and now we were cleared to descend. Aboe gently eased the nose over, then slowly retarded the throttles to ensure he didn't disrupt the airflow into the engines enough to cause a compressor stall. By this time, we had pierced the veil of clouds from the storm. Now no longer blind, we could actually see where we were headed, and it was clear sailing ahead for us. This allowed us to close the engine anti-ice valves and bring the throttles to the idle setting. And they needed to be at idle because we had popped out of the weather around thirty-five miles north of the field. Arrivals were landing south on runway

15R. This meant we were extremely high for the approach, so Bob pointed the nose straight down. This was not your standard descent profile, but we needed to lose about thirty-five thousand feet in thirty-five miles. Straight down worked for us.

ATC switched us over to approach control as we were approaching ten thousand feet. Aboe had already extended the speed brake as we began to slow to three hundred knots before we continued the descent. Three hundred knots was our maximum allowable airspeed below ten thousand feet, and we had a lot more speed than that to get rid of before we could go any lower. The aircraft was shaking and shuddering in protest. We were asking it to go against its nature by demanding it to both quickly slow down and go down. It wasn't designed to do this, and the only way to achieve the results being demanded from it was by extending a big piece of flat, unattractive metal from the aircraft's underbelly into the airstream. It was an affront to its sleekness, grace, and beauty. The moderate buffeting we were experiencing was its derisive response to our demands. Nevertheless, we needed the speed brake, even after we finally slowed enough to press lower. We were still too high.

Approach control cleared us to continue our descent for a visual straight-in approach to runway 15R when we checked in with them. I backed up Aboe by tuning in the Instrument Landing System (ILS) for 15R in the navigation radio. It would provide up, down, left, and right guidance to a point on the runway one thousand feet from its approach end. We finished all the descent checklist items in time, retracted the speed brake, and prepared for landing. Hard to believe, but we were successful in losing all that altitude without extensive vectoring by approach control.

And we had successfully dealt with Reese being closed for our arrival without fuel becoming an issue at our new destination. Time to congratulate ourselves and pat ourselves on the back for being the superior airmen that we were? Not quite yet.

The T-38 is almost flawless in its design and engineering. It was initially conceived in 1959 by the gifted engineers of Northrup Corporation, aided with little more than graph paper and slide rules. The result was a classic design that has withstood the test of time. The first one rolled off the production line in 1961, and Air Force pilot trainees are fortunate enough to still be flying it today. But it's not quite perfect, and we were about to deal with one of those imperfections.

The canopy defogger system in the T-38, under ordinary use, oftentimes proved to be ineffective. In our particular circumstances, starting with our near-freefall from forty-seven thousand feet and a seriously cold-soaked canopy, to configuring on final in the hot, humid aftermath of the storm, resulted in completely overwhelming the system. The forward canopy of the aircraft fogged up, and Aboe was flying blind again. My seat in the rear cockpit sits slightly higher than the forward cockpit, and my side views were clearer, so I offered to take over and land. It looked like all the "practice" of landing from the back seat in case of a front-seat emergency was about to pay off. Fortunately, Aboe's side views from the canopy were clear enough that he felt he could land the jet. Bob would just fly the ILS down and flare using the side views, similar to the way we landed from the back seat. It worked out for us. He did a superb job shooting the approach and touching down, but we would both continue to "practice" our backseat landings. You never knew when you might be called upon to step up and perform when the situation demanded it.

We cleared the runway, relieved to be on the ground as we taxied toward the transient ramp in front of Base Ops. We had already opened our canopies and were breathing in the warm air of North Texas; glad the stress of the flight was behind us. Neither of us had been to Sheppard before. Keeping with the day we were having, the base was about to welcome us with one more surprise.

Airborne diversions to alternate fields are always messy affairs, and this one proved messier than most. The crew chief on the ramp marshaled us to our parking spot, a good distance from the Base Ops building, and gave us the signal to stop. Bob complied, then shut down the engines. Our crew chief quickly chocked the wheels as we began to finish up the last few items on the engine-shutdown checklist. Since I was in the back seat, I was in charge of filling out the aircraft forms. It didn't take long before I put them aside and was unstrapping from my seat and parachute, standing up, and stretching after our long, stressful flight. Aboe was doing the same thing when we both noticed a big, four-door Ford painted Air Force blue with a white top racing toward us from our right side. Very few people are given the authority to drive such cars, especially on the aircraft ramps of Air Force bases, and just to confirm what we already suspected, we now could see the eagle insignia framed by the license-plate holder of the car. We were the only aircraft on the ramp, so it looked like Bob and I were about to meet the wing commander of the 82nd Training Wing at Sheppard Air Force Base. And from the way he was accelerating toward us, it was unlikely we would be getting a friendly handshake and a fruit basket in honor of our first visit.

The big Ford skidded to stop about twenty yards in front of our aircraft nose. The driver had already put the car's transmission into park because as the car was sliding forward, the driver-side door was swinging open, and the driver was stepping out of his vehicle. And what was emerging from the vehicle was nothing less than a six-foot, four-inch, two-hundred-fifty-pound full colonel, complete with a flattop haircut and a fat cigar between his lips. He stood there on the ramp glaring at us for a second. Then he took the cigar out of his mouth, shouting over to us, "ARE YOU THE T-38 THAT GOT HAIL DAMAGE FROM THE THUNDERSTORM?!"

Hail? This was the first time we had heard of any aircraft receiving hail damage by the thunderstorm. Not even when we were being vectored by ATC or when we were on approach control was there any mention of a crippled aircraft or even hail itself. We instinctively looked at our wings to make sure we were not the subjects of this angry colonel's search. Thankfully, they were as sleek, clean, and unblemished by hail as ever. Relieved but still apprehensive, we said it wasn't us. The huge, imposing colonel continued to glare at us for a moment, then stuck the cigar back in his mouth as he pivoted back to his vehicle. He would have to look elsewhere to find this stricken aircraft so he could have a friendly chat with the crew. He quickly reentered his car, slammed the door shut, gunned the engine, and raced off without another word.

"Welcome to Sheppard," I thought as "Colonel Hospitality" sped away in his big blue and white "welcome wagon." Some T-38 pilots' bad day was only going to get worse once he found them. Still, they had one silver lining in the horrible, dark cloud of their day today. At least they didn't have to explain what happened to their aircraft to Joel. Big and imposing as he was, the colonel wasn't Joel, and they weren't flying Joel's aircraft.

Perhaps it was twenty years later when I was relating this story of my first flight to Sheppard to a small group of colleagues during a midnight hub turn in Memphis. We were eating at the hub facility's cafeteria, and I finished up the story of our meeting with the wing commander, Col. Hospitality. So, you can imagine my surprise to learn one of my dinner companions was offering to finish the story for me. And I am so glad he made the offer because there was a lot left to tell. He was commissioned two years behind me at CSU and attended pilot training at Vance AFB, less than two hundred miles north of Sheppard in Oklahoma. He knew my story wasn't finished because that crippled T-38 came from Vance, where he was an instructor pilot at the time.

As you would expect, Col. Hospitality found the T-38 with the hail damage on his base, and it wasn't a pretty sight. It was recorded as a Class-A incident, meaning $100,000 or more in damage to the aircraft. It was an IP and her student involved in the report. My friend didn't share any of the circumstances of how she ended up at Sheppard. She might have been on a student cross-country, or they were unable to recover at Vance before the thunderstorm closed down their base as it did to Reese. Regardless of how it happened, it was a very bad day for her and her student. Yet, she was the instructor pilot, so she bore the responsibility for the damage.

These kinds of incidents in your official Air Force files will oftentimes kill a career. Accident boards are convened to investigate, and it's not unusual in such circumstances that a pilot's wings, the ones we all worked so hard to earn, are revoked. In this case that did not happen.

From what I assume to be the low point in her career as an Air Force pilot, this woman, handicapped with this incident on her record, somehow found a way to become the first female to both pilot and command a NASA space shuttle. She even retired from the Air Force, having achieved the same rank as Col. Hospitality, the man so intent on finding her and her damaged aircraft back at Sheppard that day. It speaks to her character that she managed to recover from this massive career setback and achieve a singular, spectacular career. As baseball great and sage of the common man Yogi Berra famously said, "It ain't over 'til it's over." And for those willing to accept their failures and mistakes, learn from them, and work not only to avoid but grow from them, a way towards personal redemption can always be found, even during the darkest of times.

CHAPTER 12
From Right Seat to Left Seat

So, once again, I was back in the squadron and its familiar routine. Every third week would be spent on alert, starting on Thursday with crew changeovers in the morning. After spending seven days, mostly in the alert compound, we were given three-and-a-half days off, which I used to fly the T-38, mostly with Aboe as my partner.

But those three-and-a-half days in the T-38 seemed to go by too quickly, and Monday morning would find us back in the squadron doing mission planning for a tanker sortie the following day. During the next two weeks, we might fly two more times, collecting ten or twelve hours of total tanker flying time. Then it was back on alert for another seven days. For copilots to upgrade to the left seat required a minimum of 750 hours of total flying time with no fewer than 500 hours in the tanker. SAC desperately wanted the squadrons of its northern, remote bases to upgrade copilots to aircraft commanders. This avoided the exorbitant costs involved when transferring personnel from southern bases. It also avoided the issue of forcing an aircraft commander to choose between North Dakota and the civilian world. The Air Force oftentimes didn't win that contest. So, the T-38 hours were vital to upgrade strategy. Without the T-38 to help reach that 750-hour minimum threshold, it could take six years for a copilot to upgrade, past his initial Air Force commitment.

I explain all this because by this time, more than two years had passed since I had arrived at Grand Forks, and I was one of the more senior copilots in the squadron. Our crew was surprised with another deployment to RAF Fairford in England and Saudi Arabia but with a different aircraft commander. This meant spending Christmas in Riyadh again, but at least this time I had sunblock.

Upon returning to North Dakota, I found myself approaching the five-hundred-minimum-tanker-hour requirement to upgrade. I had nearly twice that amount in the T-38, so the squadron was just waiting for my tanker hours to reach the minimum. I was told this by the OPS officer one afternoon in his office. He also mentioned that they were going to upgrade me locally rather than send me back to Castle AFB in California where I first became acquainted with the Strategic Air Command and the KC-135. This was bittersweet news because I would lose the privilege of flying the T-38 once I moved to the left seat, but I could still fly it while doing upgrade training at Grand Forks. Coming out of his office, I thought, "Well, things could be worse. Even though I have to upgrade to aircraft commander, I don't have to endure another trip to Castle AFB, and I still have some time left in the T-38." Wouldn't you know it? In a couple of weeks, things got worse.

The reason for my being upgraded in-house at Grand Forks was a copilot slightly junior to me was given the Castle slot. All squadrons had to keep minimum manning requirements to be listed as mission-ready, and manning was so thin in our squadron the staff could not afford to send two copilots to upgrade at once. So, he was going. I would stay and still be officially listed as a copilot during the local upgrade program. This individual blew up those plans when he was credibly accused of making a false claim to be an aircraft commander in the KC-135 (the military equivalent to the Boeing 707) on his FAA pilot type-certification application for the Boeing 707. The FAA takes these type ratings very seriously. When their Fargo office did an investigation and discovered he hadn't even started left-seat training at Castle AFB, they were not amused. They felt they were being played for fools and informed the squadron. The squadron leadership wanted him court-martialed, and a formal investigation was started. In the meantime, there was an opening for their Castle slot. I did my best to convince the OPS officer to send someone else and let me keep the local upgrade, but I lost the argument. So, I was going to train in California after all. The original instigator of this problem eventually beat the court martial, but it was obvious to everyone, had he just waited another six months, he would have gotten the FAA rating legally. Why he couldn't wait, he would never say. My thought was that he was born and raised in New Jersey, and with all that in his background, he just couldn't help himself.

So, plans had changed, and I was going to attend the SAC formal upgrade program in central California. To prepare me for success, the squadron was going to give me a series of ten flights in the left seat so I could at least be familiar with using my right hand on the throttles and taxiing the aircraft by the time I got there. We missioned-planned for the first sortie with me acting as an aircraft commander and the instructor pilot in the role of copilot.

The next morning when we arrived, the weather was horrible across most of the country. We had takeoff and landing minimums but not much more, and our alternate landing base was Carswell AFB near Dallas, Texas, about three-and-a-half hours away. So we went through our preflight checklists, started the engines, taxied out, configured, and were cleared for takeoff. The visibility was bad but still legal as we rolled down the runway and rotated. Once airborne, I called for gear up, and the IP was unable to raise the gear handle. A safety switch on the landing gear was preventing it from being brought up by the gear handle in the cockpit in case it wasn't hanging properly before retraction. If it wasn't hanging properly before being raised, you could end up severing some important hydraulic lines while adding some new holes in your aircraft's underbelly. This would not be a great way to start my first left-seat ride.

I was in the weather almost from rotation, so I kept hand-flying and directed the IP to get out the appropriate checklist while I sent the boom operator back to examine the landing gear through portholes in the floor specifically designed for just such an emergency. He came back saying it was a stuck safety switch, not a hanging-gear problem. We were clear to override the gear handle and raise the gear. This was fortunate because we would not have the fuel to reach Dallas with hanging gear if the visibility grew worse. The gear came up using the override trigger on the gear handle, and on we pressed. For about a minute. That was about how long it took to get the gear up before the number-four engine fire light illuminated. At that point, I was asking myself half-jokingly if the IP was trying to make this flight into an emergency procedure simulator. No matter, I took charge. Air Traffic Control called to clear us to a higher altitude. I had the IP declare an emergency and request a descent to approach altitude in preparation for a return to the field. We then ran the checklists, shut down the number four engine, coordinated with the command post and the receiver, and configured the aircraft for our final approach. Just outside the outer marker fix, I asked the IP if he wanted to take over the controls for landing. After all, it was an emergency landing, and he had signed for the airplane. But he said no, the landing was mine. I didn't argue. I hand-flew the approach and was able to pick up the runway approach lights through the fog just above decision height. This allowed me to continue the approach for an uneventful touchdown and rollout.

Flights like these require even more paperwork than normal. When we got back to the squadron, the IP put me in charge of it and disappeared while I dealt with it all. It was more than I imagined for such a short flight. So, I sat down and focused on ensuring all the paperwork was correct, glumly realizing this would be a big part of my new role as aircraft commander. I had just completed the last form and was sitting there, casually reviewing the inch-high stack of paperwork in front of me when the IP showed up. I asked how he managed to return just as I finished with all those forms, and he said knowing how comes with experience. We both laughed, and then he said we had to go see the OPS officer in his office.

So, the IP and I went directly from the squadron flight planning room to the office. We walked in, and the IP closed the door behind us, making me wonder what was coming next. We sat down, and the OPS officer looked at me with something more like a grimace than a smile on his face, smartly slapped the tops of his thighs with his hands, and announced, "You're done!" I was puzzled by what he meant, and it must have shown on my face. I asked what he was referring to by being done, and he said, "You're done with the training program for upgrade." I soon figured out that meant all the extra left-seat flights I was scheduled for would be replaced with more time on alert. So, no good deed goes unpunished, at least in our squadron.

Soon enough, I was off to Castle AFB in California, this time for left-seat training, but I wanted to detail that upgrade training experience because it became emblematic of my entire aviation career spanning civilian and military flying. That would not be the only time I had to shut down an engine in flight. It was only the first of five: two in the KC-135, one in the RC-135, and two in the Boeing 727. They are characteristically a rare experience unless I happen to be in the cockpit. I also had a number of airborne cargo fire indications (fortunately, all false), airborne loss of main hydraulics a couple of times, stuck flight controls, smoke in the cabin (I came close to opening my cockpit window on final approach to deal with the smoke), loss of cabin pressure numerous times, complete loss of my Flight Management System on the A-300 (the most fulfilling of all the emergencies I experienced because I hand-flew that beast completely from Omaha to Memphis with only basic flight instruments). There were so many more, but the intent of this missive is not about chronicling these incidents. It is about faith and choice. I chose to write about this experience to showcase what it was I unwittingly said yes to back in my freshman year of high school. Sometimes a lot is asked of you, but nothing more than you can handle. More on that later.

I came back from Castle AFB and was assigned to a crew. Before I left, I had worked on my own with the Management Personnel Center to request an assignment to Offutt AFB in the RC-135. I wanted to be near my favorite softball player. The assignment came through before I left for California, and after about six months from the upgrade, I left North Dakota to fly the reconnaissance version of the C-135. This meant moving back to the copilot's seat because of the mission but also learning how to be on the back end of the air refueling process. Much more exciting and challenging. Moving back to the right seat once again qualified me to fly the T-38, also stationed at Offutt. So, things were falling in place for me with my move south to Omaha: my favorite softball player, more flying time, and a more challenging mission, back in the T-38. Life wasn't just good. It was great!

Flying the RC-135 meant I would usually deploy for forty-five days at a stretch. It was a great mission, especially during the Cold War, and we flew so much that I would log almost ten times as many hours a month as I would back in my old tanker squadron. Yet, by this time, your mother and I were getting serious about a life together and being deployed six to eight months a year is not exactly a life together. So, we became engaged unofficially. I informed the Air Force I was separating from the service and surprised her with the engagement ring at my separation party on the day I left the Air Force. My mother and father were there, and they were thrilled. They truly loved Denise as it showed over time.

CHAPTER 13
A Changing of Uniforms

I left the Air Force in July of 1984. By October, I was starting class to fly for a small but aggressive start-up carrier called People Express, domiciling out of Newark, New Jersey. Your mother and I planned for a September wedding the following year. In the interim, I was living in New Jersey and jump-seating home as often as I could.

One day I received a letter from my mother at my New Jersey address. Denise and I had already agreed to get married in the Catholic Church out of respect for my parents. They were not yet aware of this, but they were very aware that I had "fallen away from the Church." Mom was writing with her concerns about not engaging in the sacrament of matrimony officiated by a priest. And your grandmother was a gifted writer. In such wonderful prose, she expressed their love for both of us, how much and how deeply both she and Dad had been praying for this wonderful union and for me to return to the faith. God had been involved in my life, whether I was willing to acknowledge it or not. It was important not just to them but to me and Denise to start our life together with His blessing.

I returned to Omaha on the jump seat soon enough so I could tell them face-to-face of our plans to get married in the Church. They were so happy to hear the news. Denise and I met with the priest at St. James, where I was an altar boy long ago, and signed up for the marriage classes with Father Fitzgerald, the pastor at the time. We took the marriage-compatibility test and found we had nearly identical values, differing only on religion. Your mother was brought up as a Baptist, so she needed "sum schoolin" before she took her wedding vows in a Catholic ceremony. Since I was already Catholic and hardly in town, I could skate on class attendance, but, in truth, I could have benefited from it more than your mother. I was prideful: sometime earlier when we were discussing faith, I told your grandmother that everything I had accomplished I had done on my own through intelligence, drive, and determination. And although I didn't say it, I thought I had a pretty respectable list of accomplishments, the primary one being I was still hanging around so I could assemble a list. But I was caught up in the heat of the moment back then. I had totally overlooked my "voice directives" when I was responding to your grandmother's queries about personal faith. Her letter was a wonderfully gentle rebuttal to these remarks, telling me I had more help than I realized. I wasn't quite ready to accept her reasoning and maternal concern on this subject. But it helped to plant a seed for the proper time, which was sooner now rather than later.

CHAPTER 14
Faith Reborn

So, your mother and I were married in September of 1985, and as I have often reminded her since then, it was the best decision I ever made. How empty my life would have been without her. Seventeen months after we took our vows, Matthew arrived. Finally, my willingness to accept an Almighty Presence, a true Creator who bound His universe with physical laws, a natural order, and immense beauty was here. Our son was born. Because of that, my faith was reborn.

Yet I would not be honest if I claimed this to be a road-to-Damascus moment, with my faith completely restored after a blinding flash of light. For one, St. Paul's circumstances were a little different from mine. More to the point, as I stated much earlier, the roots of my faith weren't all that deep to begin with. I purposely chose to say my faith was merely reborn, not restored, to even that meager depth. Like our new son, it had to be carefully nurtured and fed to grow, and it would take more time. I began with small, reasoned steps, accepting the universe and its laws had to have a beginning, and that beginning necessitated a Master Craftsman to design and create it. St. Thomas Aquinas referred to this principle as a First Cause. It was enough to start me attending Mass again. But I attended Mass bringing a lot of skepticism with me through the church doors. Our son, so beautifully, wonderfully constructed, filled with potential, was our own personal miracle. But a virgin birth and other supposed miracles from two thousand years earlier were, to me, a bit too much to swallow. I paid close attention to the service, particularly the epistle, the gospel, and the homily. Yet even with twelve years of Catholic education, other parts of the Mass left me mystified as to their purpose. In short, I was still a work in progress when it came to my spiritual life.

Eight months after Matthew's arrival, I changed employers from People Express in Newark to Federal Express (FedEx) in Memphis. It turned out to be a game-changer for our new and growing family as well.

Federal Express was a much smaller company when I started. That and the fact much of the flying was at night kept it off the desirability lists of many pilots. Yet in Grand Forks, I had begun an interest in the stock market, learning to access and read a company's balance sheet and estimate potential. When I looked at Federal Express as a possible employer, I saw their potential for growth was huge. One respected industry analyst had written about the coming shake-up in the airline industry due to deregulation. There were only two certain survivors in his estimation: one was United Airlines, and the other was FedEx. At that time, FedEx had fewer than one thousand pilots compared with United Airlines' ten thousand. I felt extremely fortunate to be there, and with my past work experience at the bakery, I handled night flying better than most.

As an added benefit, FedEx had Omaha layovers in its domestic flight schedule. It took a while to achieve the seniority to hold the Omaha line. Still, once I could, I was able to layover during the day and fly out at night, only to return the next morning. Sometimes I wouldn't see any other layover city for a couple of months at a time. This started around the time our wonderful daughter Erin arrived. We were twice blessed with intelligent, beautiful, healthy children. We felt so fortunate! The extra time at home made our life together seem more normal than that of your typical airline pilot, especially one who commuted. I was deeply grateful and hoped you appreciated it too, even if I sometimes embarrassed either of you by showing up at a school event in my FedEx uniform.

Yet I wasn't always able to layover at home. Monthly schedules for aircraft layovers changed, as did my ability to hold Omaha with my changes in seat position. When I found myself laying over for weekends in unfamiliar cities and unable to attend Sunday services, I came up with the idea of packing a Bible to help continue my religious education. Since I realistically couldn't attend Mass for the Scripture readings and homilies, time with the Bible would have to do. I made the effort to read something from the New Testament on such Sundays, and it sparked a lot of confusion at first, followed by curiosity. There were baffling stories coming from its pages like the healing of the demoniac near the shore of Sea of Galilee, where two thousand possessed pigs ended up drowning themselves in the water, according to Luke's gospel. Matthew's gospel offers a similar account of the events on the seashore but mentions two, rather than one demoniac. Or the man with the withered hand miraculously being healed in a synagogue on the Sabbath and the rage felt by the scribes and Pharisees after they were a witness to this. Perhaps the most perplexing problem for me was Christ's twelve traveling companions. Was He really counting on these guys to carry on His legacy after His planned exit from public ministry? Other than His rising from the dead, I figure this must be the biggest miracle of all the New Testament after reading through the gospels. Those twelve did not inspire confidence, to be frank.

These kinds of Sunday layover readings and regular church attendance, listening to scripture being spoken, and the homilies that followed piqued my interest more. I bought a more comprehensive Bible that included theological discussions of scripture passages by respected theologians and Doctors of the Church, quite a thick version of Catholic Cliff Notes. Sometimes while reading, I felt the same kind of intellectual rush I had when I was studying back in college. I could lose myself in it for long periods of time.

Naturally, at some point, I had to ask myself what it was I was doing here. All this reading, studying, and even analyzing a book that at key times had all four contributors of the gospels describe an event, and they could not agree on who was there and what was said. At least you would think they could get the Lord's Prayer right, but the two who wrote it down each gave their own version of it. Why should I have any faith in it? It had too many contradictions, especially for a book that claimed divine inspiration for all four gospel writers.

Yet, two thousand years later, we still feel the impact of this carpenter's son on history, even after He was brutally executed by the authorities and His followers went into hiding to avoid the same fate. Reviewing antiquity, I couldn't find any similar instance of a messianic cult leader preaching nonviolence who predicted his manner of execution by the authorities and promising to return "on the third day." Talk about setting yourself up for failure. Yet after His death, His movement grew instead of drying up like those past cult leaders. Rather than the teachings from such individuals becoming no more than a footnote in history, His became the basis for the most widely printed book ever. Where the followers of earlier cult leaders scattered and disappeared after their leader's demise, there are presently almost 1.4 billion baptized Catholics worldwide all these centuries later. All these followers came from a group of twelve men, one who gave their leader over to His captors, ten who fled, and an adolescent boy who stayed at the foot of His cross to watch that leader die ignominiously. What are the odds of a religion being born and sustained to the present day from such a chaotic inception? I can't exactly quantify it, so the best answer I could offer is "not very good."

Despite such long odds, we find ourselves dealing with just such a reality. Could this faith in the teachings of an enemy of the scribes and Pharisees, not to mention Rome, survive two thousand years, beating such immeasurably large odds by its existence and still be just a hoax or misunderstanding? I had to ask that question. Logically speaking, it is possible—incredibly unlikely, but possible. The other choice was that it was true despite some inconsistencies in the telling of its history, and those twelve apostles, minus the traitor, took to heart their resurrected leader's instruction to "Go and make disciples of all nations." They proceeded to evangelize the world with a great deal of help through divine intervention, curing the sick, raising the dead, casting out demons, and more, just like their religious founder, invoking His name each time they performed such an act. Pretty much that is the choice between a hoax or misunderstanding, and divinely nurtured faith we all face. It is not an easy choice, but it still must be made, and consequences follow from whatever we decide.

So, I continued to attend Mass, read, listened, and learned. I tried straddling the fence with agnosticism for a while, but it proved too difficult for me. I was trying to exist each day in that thin seam of twilight between the darkness, finality, and isolation of the secular world, and the bright, everlasting joy promised by the Christian world to those who follow Christ's teachings. Not only did this daily struggle prove unsatisfying for me, but it was leading nowhere. I reasoned that life is defined by the choices we make and choosing not to choose on life's most defining question would lead to a wasted life. I eventually chose Christ, the Church, and its sacraments.

To give you an idea of how long this process took, I made a long overdue confession the day before I married your mother in 1985. It wasn't until December 18, 2015, after I retired from FedEx, that I once again received the sacrament of reconciliation. In this case, the math is easy—thirty years. But what a spiritually tortuous path I took during those thirty years, and if I was being honest, really dating all the way back to college. The good news is even though it took a while, I rediscovered there is a God. He makes demands of us all, but we have free will to choose whether to accept those demands or reject them. Consequences follow from whichever choice we make. More good news. He is a loving, caring God, patient with us up to the very last moment of life, and there is evidence of possibly even beyond that. So never give up hope.

Epilogue

In Hebrews 11:1 (ESV) it states, "Faith is the assurance of things hoped for, the conviction of things not seen." Apparently, God had a lot more faith in me than I did in Him. Starting with my freshman year in high school, I was given several assurances from the Almighty. Be an airline pilot. Join the Air Force. Go to CSU. Get your grades up or forget about UPT. Sign the commissioning letter. You will get your slot. Say hello to SAC and North Dakota, flyboy. You really should play softball today. I paraphrase a bit, but in each case my response barely made the threshold for a passing grade and certainly could not be viewed as being done with a strong conviction of faith. Nevertheless, I did what was asked of me. Why was it asked of me in particular? After years of reflection, I cannot give you a certain answer as to why I was chosen. But I can say on assignment night for our UPT class I was sent to Grand Forks AFB to fly a KC-135 so I could save the lives of my fellow crewmembers. Perhaps as my reward, I was directed to play softball one afternoon. What is important to note is I did what was asked of me, all the while refusing to seriously question the source of my career aspirations. So, if you are struggling with religious faith or even the concept of an eternal being, believe me, I understand. I look back at all the extraordinary help given to me, and the best I can say about my faith is I was a most reluctant servant. Had I not received any direction and was left to my own devices, I probably would have ended up another lost soul—and perhaps that is why I was given extra help. But I can only speculate.

I eventually came to my senses and acknowledged privately that this actually happened to me. That acknowledgement put me on the path to regaining faith in the Almighty enough to finally put down those strong roots in rich soil spoken about in Matthew's gospel. Now I am sharing my story with you so you also may come back to your faith if you haven't already.

But if you are a bit skeptical of my ability to accurately recall all these events after such a long time, I can understand. My premise for faith in a loving God has pretty much been a personal experience with half-a-dozen low-grade voice commands. Not exactly a resounding proof of miraculous, divine intervention that turns belief solely in scientific law and critical reasoning upside down. Objectively speaking, it's just as plausible that I have been fooling myself all these years and have been really lucky beating some long odds.

So, I am asking you to do me a few favors. The first is to look up the story of a WWI British soldier named John Traynor. You can find it on Google easily. He is one of the seventy-one officially sanctioned miracles of healing from the Baths of Lourdes in France.

Secondly, I ask you to review the battery of scientific tests that have been performed on the Shroud of Turin, the cloth that draped over the crucified body of Christ in the tomb. You can find that at crediblecatholic.com if you are looking for a place to start. A number of highly regarded scientists in a wide range of disciplines have only a speculative idea of how the figure of a body was cooked onto a linen cloth about nineteen hundred years before there was even electricity, yet alone lasers. Initially, it will be dull reading, but it has a gripping climax.

Lastly, just read from Luke 15:11-32, the Parable of the Prodigal Son. Somewhere in my studies of the New Testament I read that if Jesus, during His public ministry, only told one parable to His followers, it would have been this one. Pay attention to what the father does when he sees his son in the distance, something very uncharacteristic for patriarchs of the time. Then reflect on what you have learned from my story and your "homework."

Remember, Jesus said, "Destroy this temple and in three days I will raise it up." If He wasn't kidding about that, He probably wasn't kidding about all the other things He said either.

Afterword

You may be puzzled by finding an afterword following the story's epilogue. After all, an epilogue usually serves as a conclusion, sometimes including some commentary like mine does. But I wanted to take the epilogue in a certain direction, and what follows doesn't belong in the narrative or quite fit in the epilogue. An afterword is the best I can come up with to take care of a few remaining issues.

So, looking back, I have to say it's been quite the story. I wanted to get it down on paper for you, as I stated in the prologue, hoping my witness to the faith would encourage you to come back to the Church and its sacraments. My mother's letter to me while I was living in New Jersey was important to my return. I hope my few pages (okay, several pages, maybe more than several pages) of ruminations on my life and God's hand in it will provide the spark for you to come back. And if you're wondering if I had another voice experience, this time telling me to get my affairs in order, the answer is no. I am quite healthy. But I just celebrated my sixty-sixth birthday, and I must acknowledge there is more runway behind me than ahead of me. Better to do it now rather than later.

Perhaps another thing you were wondering about from this story, going all the way back to 1970 and my first experience with the quiet voice is, why an airline pilot? After all, a message to a fifteen-year-old boy and the message is, "Be an airline pilot." You would think the directive would more likely be toward ordination and the priesthood. But an airline pilot? Not exactly a professional group known for their strong religious convictions that would inspire people toward God. More likely, from my forty years of experience in aviation, it would be to point them in the opposite direction. So why the unusual choice? This was a stumbling block for me on my path to accepting my additional help in (shall we call it) "career planning," and my slow pivot back toward the Church.

Why did it happen this way? After a good bit of time involving the recollection of the events I described, along with some reflection, I came up with an explanation. I cannot claim it's the answer because what we are dealing with in this story can never offer absolute certainty when it comes to the truth, at least on this side of the grave. But it does offer a plausible explanation if you're willing to accept the kind of faith Hebrews calls for mentioned in the epilogue. So please bear with me.

As I stated earlier, I had heard before assignment night back in UPT that I was going to fly a KC-135 in a Northern Tier base. It turned out I was needed in Grand Forks because an aircraft commander was ill-suited for his position. Still, the challenge for me was not just in the airplane but also for my faith. There were times in the cockpit I really had my hands full to ensure a safe outcome for our crew, but my struggle with faith proved to be even more of a challenge. I was given some foreknowledge of events to help with acceptance of a Divine presence in my life when the time finally arrived to squarely confront my faithlessness. But before I could arrive at that point, I first needed to arrive at Grand Forks, and this would prove to be no easy task. Earlier in the narrative I stated that sometimes a lot is asked of you, but never more than you can handle. In my case, the challenge was no more than I could handle but no less, either. It arrived as our flight was standing at attention for our first day on the T-37 flightline and didn't end until we were dismissed on our last day of T-37 training. Thankfully, I was offered earlier challenges in my life to strengthen my resolve and prepare me for that five-month ordeal. Otherwise, I doubt I would have lasted a month before I became one more training failure from E-Flight, Reese Air Force Base, Class of 79-03.

The most difficult of these pre-flightline challenges was collecting seventy-five-pound hay bales for winter storage during the hot Nebraska summer. As a wiry sixteen-year-old, I walked beside an old, slow-moving tractor pulling a flatbed trailer, lifting and stacking those hay bales, acre after acre, with leather gloves as my only aid. I was being paid a dollar an hour for my efforts, so my career as a ranch hand only lasted the summer.

A close second in preparatory challenges was operating the molder during my college years as a baker. The molder was a hulking, difficult piece of 1930s industrial technology designed to marry bread dough to half-a-dozen welded bread pans in a very quick ceremony. Big dough balls were separately spit out onto a fast-moving conveyor belt and sped through guides to roll and shape each one before they were dropped into their respective pans. It was only a matter of seconds before all six pans were filled, and the unit was lifted off the end of the molder, placed on a large, heavy, awkward bread rack that was pushed aside with a great effort once it was filled. When a few seconds were available, empty bread racks needed to be retrieved and positioned for use. The filled racks also needed to be shoved into the "hot box" to help the yeast rise at a quicker pace. In the meantime, the bread pans kept filling up and being released from the end of the molder. This process went on throughout the night, and it required strength, speed, and planning to keep the molder operating and the production line running smoothly. My first night on the molder was about as successful as Lucy Ricardo (Lucille Ball's character) and Ethel Mertz's (Lucy's friend) experience on the production line of the chocolate candy factory. It's a comedy classic available on the internet if you are not familiar with it. Unfortunately for me and my fellow production line workers, on that night I was not only familiar with the scene; I was also living it. I can laugh now at both their performance and mine, but I certainly wasn't laughing my first night of being in charge of the molder.

These two challenges, along with emptying box cars loaded with one-hundred-pound bags of sugar, one bag at a time, for storage in the bakery basement, and my academic "full-court press," were important events in my life. They were all difficult, demanding tasks that needed to be accomplished, and if I failed or chose to walk away from any one of them, it would have left a lasting impression on me—and not a very good one. They came to me as gifts, wrapped in physical and mental challenges in preparation for our time spent on the T-37 flightline. I needed every last one of them, but if someone at the time told me, "This challenge is for your own good," I might have responded by hitting them in the mouth—if I had any strength left to do it. Yet, time and reflection have revealed how important and generous gifts they really were. When we were younger, our father always had a ready response to our complaints and pleadings for him to relent when he would assign an "onerous" task around the house for us to accomplish. His gentle, but firm reply would be, "It builds character." Not only was the decision settled with his pronouncement, but time vindicated his wisdom. These four challenges, in particular, provided me with enough "character" to survive my time on the T-37 flightline, though just barely.

The other piece of this airline career choice puzzle I wrote about was meeting your mother. It turns out that her life as an Air Force dependent soured her on a life as an Air Force wife. With the help of the quiet voice, I knew where this relationship was headed, and I decided to get an early start on our future together. I opened a discussion with her about coming up to North Dakota while I was still a copilot in Grand Forks. I was preparing to discuss marriage with her when she just sweetly smiled at me and said she had spent most of her life as an Air Force dependent. She knew what Air Force life was like, and she wasn't interested in being around Air Force wives, especially officers' wives. Besides, she liked her job, and there probably wasn't anything comparable to it in Grand Forks. Well, that short discussion didn't quite go like I hoped or planned. Good thing I hadn't arranged for a moving van.

It turns out this was the right call for us. With all the T-38 flying plus the RC-135 time I logged once I transferred to Offutt AFB, I became a highly qualified candidate for any major carrier. Had she come up to North Dakota, it may have proved more difficult to leave for us. It also shows that I needed to trust in Providential plans back in Lubbock, Texas, on assignment night when I was fuming about a KC-135 to Grand Forks. So, rather than hearing about simply being an Air Force pilot back when I was a freshman in high school, I was told to be an airline pilot. I am sure I have your mother to thank for that.

God got a two-fer out of me. He sent me to North Dakota on a mission and then arranged for me and your mother to meet. That meeting led to both of you, the best part of this whole story. Words cannot express how much we love and cherish you.

Getting this all down on paper has been a difficult, demanding task spread over the better part of a year. It also has been a wonderful challenge for me. I am so happy to share the fruits of this labor with you and hope you come back to your faith. He will always be ready to forgive and accept you.

In summation, I have been blessed with a remarkable life. I have been even more blessed to have built and shared it with your mother and both of you. I love you always.

Your father
March 25, 2021

Acknowledgments

When I started planning this in the Spring of 2020, I knew I was facing a daunting project. I felt compelled to share my life experiences to help you on your own journeys through life, but to get it into a readable—yet alone believable—narrative would take some kind of effort. I am not a writer. I always left that skill to the more qualified members of the family I grew up with. Each one of them excelled at it to a much higher level than me, save one. Nevertheless, I was determined to see it through, so I began collecting my thoughts and memories trying to figure out a way to organize it into a readable, cohesive form.

I remember writing down a number of salient events from my past and trying to arrange them in some kind of order to reflect a direction and theme. That now seems humorous in a way. That fifteen-year-old kid sitting in an otherwise empty classroom was so earnest and resolute in his initial efforts to find his direction in life. Funny, he found direction. It just didn't come from him, and it came so fast he didn't have time to write any of his characteristic lists.

So here I sit over fifty years later, and I have had some help getting to this point. I want to acknowledge this help in a way that might also add to the story.

We can start with your mother. Recalling the circumstances of how we first met, it is obvious we were meant to travel through life as a couple—and we made a formidable one. We each had strengths that complemented the other. We also loved each other tremendously and trusted each other when life demanded those strengths be displayed. It's been a wonderful union. You two and the lives you have chosen are the best proof. Yet it may never have happened if it weren't for my father's health, a determination to play softball one afternoon despite the lack of skill, or even a glove, and a quart of orange juice. I mentioned the marriage-compatibility test we took before we made our vows and the near perfect match we achieved with our respective scores. I felt this small fact was important. It lends at least some credibility to my claim of being encouraged to play softball back then by someone besides Rossi.

I also have my parents to acknowledge. As far as I am concerned, I won the parental lottery jackpot. They were kind, intelligent, loving, talented people who put the four of us children ahead of everything else in life. What makes it truly remarkable is their early lives were so chaotic and dysfunctional, and yet they grew into caring, responsible adults. They met at the University of Missouri in Columbia back in the 1940s. Your grandmother was escaping from a tumultuous home life caused by an

Acknowledgments

alcoholic father who was verbally and sometimes physically abusive. She was an exceptionally bright young woman from a small farming community in central Illinois. Her younger brother, Dan, toward the end of his life, recalled for me with a hint of familial pride that her small high school class would produce three Fortune 500 CEOs. Yet your grandmother was the class valedictorian. She was able to attend college because of the generosity of a married couple who employed her at their ice cream store in her high school years. They were childless, recognized her potential, were familiar with her home life, and helped finance her education out of the kindness of their hearts. She loved writing and enrolled in the university's journalism program with the intent to use her gifts and talents while earning a steady paycheck working for a newspaper. She was determined to remain single, given her upbringing.

As awful as your grandmother's early life was, your grandfather's early years were even worse. He was the last of six children, born in 1923. His father was a lawyer in Hartington, Nebraska, and like your grandmother's father, also an alcoholic. He hanged himself in the basement of the family's home one winter's night when Dad was eleven. His mother suffered a serious mental collapse as a result and ended up in the Nebraska state mental institution for the rest of her life. Dad's existence at this point was more feral than structured. It was during the Depression and the six children, with no help from family or friends, were left to fend for themselves. They stuck together as best they could. Dad ended up living with two older sisters in Omaha after a stint in an all-girl Catholic orphanage in Nebraska City. He and the only other boy in the facility had to rise early each day to serve as altar boys for daily Mass.

Not surprisingly, Dad rarely said anything about his years growing up. The little I found out came from your grandmother one day while I was at home on break from college. She was in a reflective mood and felt like sharing our family history. She finished up her talk by telling me my grandmother passed away in the state home only a few years earlier. It was quite a somber moment for me. Not only did I find out my grandfather hanged himself when Dad was young, but my grandmother was, until a few years ago, still alive. I was led at an early age to believe she had already passed away. Mom certainly left me with a lot to think about that afternoon.

Like your grandmother, your grandfather was drawn to writing and ended up enrolling in the journalism program at the University of Missouri. He was able to afford the tuition through the GI Bill established for WWII vets. He and your grandmother shared a writing class early in their academic careers there, and after a while your grandmother was reevaluating her decision to remain single. There was no one quite like your grandfather in her high school class back in Illinois, or even in the community. They eventually married in 1950, your grandmother having to wait a year for Dad to graduate from college. He wasn't quite as dedicated to his studies as your grandmother was, disappearing from the campus for a semester or two at a time for money-making opportunities that presented themselves. Mostly these opportunities consisted of joining his older brother Jerry and his crew to sell magazines door-to-door across the country. There were other more colorful and hilarious opportunities he shared with your mother and I one evening at a family dinner, causing us to laugh so hard it brought tears to our eyes. It is easy to understand why your grandmother fell in love with him.

Acknowledgments

Still, they may have never met if it weren't for a pre-deployment physical he received just before he was to ship off to England early in WWII. According to Mom, he was on the docks waiting to board a vessel when he was pulled out of his unit and told to report to the hospital. He ended up spending a painful year there recovering and left with one less kidney. Had he shipped out, his condition might have proved too much for maritime conditions. He might have been one more casualty from a German U-boat torpedo, a bomb dropped from a Luftwaffe aircraft over England, or the Allied invasion of the Continent. After his release from the hospital, he was transferred to the administrative section of the Army Air Corps and remained stateside for the duration of WWII. One of his duties as an administrative sergeant was maintaining records of military leave time afforded to his fellow troops. Dad being Dad, he made sure his leave time was twice the amount allotted by regulation, even though the records didn't reflect it.

I treasure this story not only for revealing how humorously disdainful my father could be toward blindly following rules, regulations, and even authority. He grew up essentially an orphan with little structure in his life, surviving by intelligence and guile during the Depression. Not only did he survive, but he managed to develop a wonderful sense of humor while he was doing it. I also treasure this story because it was one of the rare stories he told us about his early years.

Brothers and sisters are important to one's development when growing up, and I was blessed to have three. Important virtues like sharing and concern for others are introduced and cultivated in the hothouse of family life. In Michigan, we lived in a small, three-bedroom, single-bath tract house that was the perfect classroom for the four of us to learn these and other wonderful attributes. Clancy, John, and I shared one bedroom, so we also had to learn how to sleep with one eye open and defend ourselves from an attack by an avenging brother during the night. We also honed the skill of eating fast at the dinner table to ensure we were sated before the food ran out. This skill had the added benefit of preventing other siblings from getting their fill from the meal, which led to some of those nighttime attacks. Poor Bridget grew up without a sister, so she never learned the skill of sleeping with one eye open. But she learned quickly to fend for herself at the dinner table despite being the youngest.

Of course, I am being facetious about this important time we spent together growing up. We have volunteered our time helping and caring for one another from childhood, following the advice and example of our wonderful parents. Your Uncle Clancy was kind enough to use his considerable editing skills to work on this project when it found its way into his mailbox unannounced. He was the first one to learn about my remarkable guidance counselor and provided much needed direction. If you find it reads well, he deserves considerable credit.

Some other people I need to acknowledge are those thirty guys who, for whatever reason, decided to give up their pilot training slots during my college years. To this day I cannot imagine what was going through their collective minds when they decided to sign the letter releasing them from any further obligation to the Air Force and forego the opportunity to attend UPT. I am extremely grateful but still puzzled.

To make my point, allow me to relate this story. One of the twenty-five students who remained in our AFROTC class

Acknowledgments

after the draft was terminated in 1973 was a pre-med student. Early in our junior year the Air Force was desperately trying to reduce the size of its pilot training pool and was handing out scholarship offers left and right to induce qualified candidates to switch career fields. My classmate could have easily swapped his pilot training scholarship for an expense-free trip through medical school, but he opted for UPT. He would rather be an Air Force pilot before he became a doctor and stubbornly clung to his flight training scholarship. As it turned out, he got his wish. He went through UPT and then went to medical school, ending up as a general and one of the country's foremost authorities on aviation physiology and medicine.

But he was like me. He was willing to sacrifice a lot for the privilege of wearing Air Force wings. I thought the rest of the 25 percent selected from our group were as dedicated to becoming pilots as we were, so when I learned I was chosen as an alternate, I was crushed. I was convinced my chances of attending UPT were almost nil. Fortunately, I followed some offered guidance and ended up being given a training slot to Reese AFB.

So, thank you again, you thirty unknown individuals. You unwittingly had a profound influence on my life, and I hope you fared well in yours. But you have no idea what you gave up.

I also need to acknowledge all the contributions my UPT classmates made toward my successful completion of pilot training and my heartfelt gratitude for their efforts. Throughout this work I have made a conscious effort to avoid filling it up with a lot of names. There were a few sprinkled in here and there. Some were mentioned because you knew them. Others were added to provide a little flavor to the story (e.g., Sister Herman). I mentioned Capt. Paul Schwemler, our T-38 flight commander, specifically because I felt he deserved an attribution for his leadership in mending our bruised and wounded flight as we arrived from T-37s. And every one of my classmates deserves similar recognition. But at this point it would just be a parade of unfamiliar names to you, nothing to distinguish them as remarkable. Yet they all really were remarkable men, on their way to considerable achievements in their lives, except for one. We had one ordained minister come from our ranks who went on to volunteer for missionary work in Cuba and Spain. Another stayed in for a twenty-plus-year career and made full colonel. Others got out early and achieved the rank of lieutenant colonel in the reserves. We had two go on to earn PhDs (one in electrical engineering from Stanford University, the other in English from Texas Christian University). One of these overachievers returned to the campus as a teacher while flying a full schedule at American Airlines. Three members became published authors. Twelve became airline captains, one being named assistant chief pilot at one point in his career.

We were fortunate to have an exceptional flight leader chaperone us through our time at Reese Air Force Base. His name was Capt. Luther "Chip" Hough. He was an Air Force Academy graduate and F-4 back-seater on his way to being the front-seater. He was also heavily blessed by God, which was crucial, given his responsibilities as our chaperone. We were a challenging group, to put it mildly.

Later in his career, Chip would become a member of the Air Force's elite Aggressor Squadron, playing the bad guy in the air while being anything but that once he unstrapped from the cockpit. He took it upon himself one day while we were fighting our way through the T-37 program to privately confront our

Acknowledgments

flight commander about his IPs' and the attrition rate of his students. We don't know exactly what was said in the meeting. Chip would never say. But it had an effect. Even though we still experienced the hostility, we were grudgingly allowed to progress through the program. I wrote in the narrative it felt like I had a target on my back almost from day one on the flightline. There's a good chance his private chat saved me from elimination. I owe him a lot, and I wasn't even aware of his sit-down with the flight commander until well after the fact. Earlier I was lamenting the lack of grown-ups to provide some oversight of E-Flight leadership. But I was wrong about my assumption. There was a grown-up in the room all along. It was Chip.

Still, we were an eclectic group with different strengths, styles, and backgrounds. We pooled all these attributes together to face our adversaries across the table from us, and it was mostly successful. We shared our individual strengths, and our buddies covered for our weaknesses. My particular strength was a modest one, and it won't come as a surprise to you. I was the designated driver on the weekends.

But to this day, we all know if we need the help of one of our classmates—if there is a threat we find ourselves facing from "across the table"—all we have to do is ask. The passage of time wouldn't change our acquired instinct to help out at all. We are that close.

Someone else who deserves to be mentioned is the aircraft commander who brought me such consternation while I was stationed in Grand Forks. I said earlier he was a good man, and I was being honest. He was very smart but modest; he always gave his best effort and tried to be a mentor for me when it came to both my faith and my Air Force career. He was very devoted to his family and together with his wife managed to raise six children while being a career Air Force officer and pilot. Their Catholic faith was an integral part of their family life. One child did not survive into adulthood due to a congenital disease. The rest went on to graduate from college and earn at least a master's degree. One ended up with a PhD in astrophysics and joined the Jesuit order as a brother. He was assigned to the Vatican as a curator of sorts for their celestial observatory in Rome. I guess the Pope needs someone to keep a close eye on the heavens, and he found the right Jesuit for the job.

I learned all this after curiosity got the better of me. I had wondered for years what became of my former boss after I was reassigned to Offutt AFB. I finally tracked down his phone number and called him during the pandemic. We talked for an hour and followed up with subsequent conversations and a wonderful lunch in Omaha while he was passing through town.

Funny how life works. After our lunch it finally occurred to me that, yes, I was assigned to his crew by a Higher Power than Management Personnel Center to ensure we kept the blue side up when we were flying. But he had much to offer me in matters of faith, and I was unwilling to listen, despite his efforts. The best I could do was attend Mass with him once or twice while we were on alert and try to change the subject when the topic of faith surfaced. In short, he was there for me just as much as I was there for him. It took me decades to realize that was the divine plan all along. But at the time, I was too short-sighted and secular to seriously entertain his inquiries. I suffered for it.

I mentioned Capt. Joel Schrimsher, the T-38 Detachment Commander at Grand Forks, and the important role he played in my life. He also influenced other young copilots as

Acknowledgments

well. There were half-a-dozen of us at the detachment who made up his "frequent flyer's club," keeping his T-38 fleet busy throughout the week. He had a light touch when it came to managing us, allowing us to learn by doing as we built up our flying time for upgrading to the left seat of the tanker or the bomber. Experience, especially in aviation, is the best teacher, and we were getting a great education in the cockpits of his aircraft.

Ironically, this educational process was threatened by our success. Our small group was flying so much that we were quickly burning through all our allotted hours assigned to the detachment. Joel came through for us, finding out the other T-38 ACE bases weren't flying nearly as much as we were and had their unused hours reassigned to us. We never had to worry about "sitting down" because we ran out of flying time for the quarter.

All the T-38 flying time proved critical for me after I left the Air Force and was interviewing for a job at FedEx. At the time, I was a Boeing 727 Flight Engineer for People Express, running the aircraft systems panel as the third crewmember in the cockpit. In the previous six months I had one hour of actual flying time in a single-engine Piper. The first part of the FedEx interviewing process took place around 12:30 a.m. in Memphis with me in the left seat of a DC-10 simulator and a line-check airman in the right seat. He had me hand-fly a set of maneuvers designed to demonstrate my precision flying skills. It was the most important simulator ride of my career, and I would have liked to have had some practice before I strapped in, but it just wasn't possible. Thankfully, all the T-38 stick time and the instrument crosscheck I developed because of it paid off.

Soon after the interviewing process was over, I had a job offer. Being assigned to Grand Forks on assignment night with Joel in charge of the ACE program there made the offer possible.

Joel's best moment for me, though, was when I received a phone call at the tanker squadron from my mother one morning. My father had suffered a heart attack, and the doctors were unsure about his survival. After exploring all my travel options to quickly return to Omaha, I went to Joel. He didn't hesitate at all to my request, sticking me in the front seat of the T-38 and another IP in the rear seat so we could fly down to Offutt. Fortunately, my dad recovered and lived another twenty years. But Joel came through when it really mattered, so thank you, Joel. You were a godsend for me and others as well at Grand Forks.

Bob Aboe is a name you are familiar with. That "short, stumpy Italian" proved to be a wonderful flying partner for me as I began my second act in the T-38. Prior to his Air Force career, Bob had enlisted in the Army. He scored high on their admittance exam, so they trained him to work in the base legal shop, previewing legal briefs for their attorneys. The training honed a natural capacity he already possessed to quickly see straight through to the core issue of a complex problem and craft a suitable solution. It also brought focus to his professional life. He decided rather than continue his career working for the Army's legal wonks perusing legal jargon, he would join the Air Force and become a fighter pilot. He almost made it, but SAC stole his dream on assignment night. After that colossal disappointment his motivation shifted to doing just enough of his tanker duties so as not to get into trouble with the squadron and to enjoy himself in the T-38.

Acknowledgments

I arrived in Grand Forks about six months after him and it seemed like he was just waiting for me to sign in at the squadron so he could get started on his new direction in life. Shortly after I was checked out in the T-38, we went on our first of many cross-country trips coming off alert. On our first day we flew five legs and logged eight hours of flying time, triggering an alarm bell in the flight records office back at Reese. It turns out there was an obscure regulation stating T-38 pilots were limited to six and a half hours of flying per day. So, from then on, we would fly four legs and log six and a half hours of flight time on our cross-countries, but they would never catch us again when it came to the rules. Aboe provided me with a first-class education in how careful reading of regulations could weaponize them to our advantage. And we were just getting started in our rule-pressing mission. Disgruntled young men oftentimes need supervision, but in our case, we had a hands-off supervisor in Joel, our T-38 detachment commander. His attitude was we alone were in charge of keeping our hard-earned Air Force wings attached to our uniforms. As long as we did nothing to endanger him or his aircraft (he sometimes referred to them as his children), we had his tacit approval. If we wanted to play in the deep end of the pool, by all means, go ahead. But we were responsible for pulling ourselves out once we dove in.

What a wonderful combination of Aboe's daring and Joel's detachment proved to be. Since we were swimming without a lifeguard, we not only determined our own actions, we also answered for them as well. And being young and overly confident in our abilities, we both pressed the limits and regularly went beyond them. We embraced this risk and ended up doing some incredibly irresponsible things, like low-level, high-speed runs through the Rockies, flying barely above the treetops as we snaked our way through the valleys or raced up to the mountain crests. Reaching the top, we would roll inverted and pull our nose down, only to roll ourselves upright as we followed the line of terrain on the downside, keeping ourselves just above the tree line. This became somewhat routine for us as we flew between Air Force bases in Great Falls, Montana, and Spokane, Washington. And it wouldn't surprise me at all if we were the cause of an avalanche or two on any of our winter trips through those mountain valleys.

These flights are just a sampling from our catalogue of many rash stunts we managed to pull off together in the T-38. Bob felt the Air Force really couldn't do him any more harm than it already had. He was a tanker copilot in Grand Forks, North Dakota. Rather than being a highly trained fighter pilot on the front lines, his skills making him the tip of the spear in wartime, he was nothing more than a gas station attendant. Was he angry about this? Of course, but there was nothing he could do about it. Despite his very best efforts in UPT to show otherwise, the Air Force had decided his particular training and skills were needed more in the right seat of a KC-135 in Grand Forks than in a fighter aircraft. So, he would oblige the Air Force and sit in that right seat. But he wasn't going to push himself to excel like he did in pilot training. Look at how all that effort was rewarded. Instead, he responded by embracing the mediocrity thrust on him by his assignment. He merely did his job, nothing more, nothing less. Where he did push himself was in the cockpit of the T-38. It definitely wasn't a fighter jet, but it was as close as he could get to one. It would have to do for now. Perhaps in a few years he could leave the active-duty Air Force, changing his position on that spear from somewhere on the shaft to the tip by joining an Air Guard or Reserve unit, and

Acknowledgments

flying a fighter jet. It was where he should have been all along. In the meantime, he would construct challenges for himself in the T-38. And he liked to challenge himself.

My motivations were different. Unlike Aboe, I deserved to be there. I barely made it through T-37s, only to find my footing in T-38s. But by that time, it was too late to recover from the damage I had done to myself. So, I ended up in Grand Forks only to be a dead man walking, or more aptly, flying. I became all but convinced it was only a matter of time before my name would be attached to an accident report as a fatality in a KC-135 crash. It occurred to me more than once that if I were caught doing something reckless in the T-38 and I lost my wings, it might actually prolong my life. Still, I hadn't been caught yet, so I would enjoy the ride while it lasted. Adrenaline can be its own addictive drug.

Yet a funny thing happened. We flew over five hundred hours together in the T-38, sometimes doing some incredibly foolish things and we were never caught doing any of them. Never! And at the risk of sounding immodest, we also became really good stick-and-rudder pilots while we were avoiding calamity with the authorities; flying on the edge of the aircraft performance envelope demands it. But as judgment goes, we were both works in progress.

There was a lot of luck involved in this. But our pressing and then exceeding the regulatory limits forced a steep learning curve to take place. We wanted to continue to play in the deep end of the pool. Temperamentally, that's where we belonged. We just had to do our best not to get caught or we would be banned from the water. Permanently. Yet sometimes those best attempts of ours to behave were woefully inadequate, our good judgment taking the day off. And that's when our large reservoir of good luck would take over. Despite our numerous attempts to drain it dry, we never succeeded.

Eventually, we both had to upgrade to the left seat of the KC-135 and leave the T-38 behind, Bob preceding me by six months. In one of our last cross-country flights together we were facing some challenging weather as we were trying to make it back to Grand Forks. The previous three legs had been equally as challenging, causing Aboe to remark jovially with one of his favorite quips, "Lesser pilots would have died!" as we were making our way home. The T-38 doesn't carry a lot of fuel, and when the ceiling or visibility is low you need an alternate landing field in case the actual weather or other factors are worse than predicted. And there weren't a lot of fields we could use with the gas we carried. Coming up with the plan proved to be an exacting task. Besides low visibility, we would be facing icing conditions in the clouds, crosswinds, and slippery runways. We were in the middle of running all the numbers we needed to file a legal flight plan when Bob looked up at me and said, "At some point, all these rules don't matter," meaning in our case, judgment takes precedence over legality. I thought to myself, "That's remarkable. I was thinking along the exact same line as him."

We quickly buried our heads again into solving our flight issues, but it proved to be a significant moment for us. It looked like all the flying in the T-38 program had finally done what it was designed to do—that is, provide young copilots the opportunity to exercise good judgment. And we caught ourselves doing just that. We were a little slower than most to figure this out.

Actually, we were a lot slower than most, weighing ourselves

Acknowledgments

down with issues that blinded us to the opportunity we were given. But we survived all those egregious lapses in judgment and came out much better for it. We were (fortunately) living proof of Nietzsche's aphorism, "What does not kill you makes you stronger." We pooled our collective skills and knowledge and made it back to Grand Forks AFB that day, working as a team. We even followed all the rules to do it.

I am sorry for Bob missing out on getting a fighter on assignment night. He definitely had the skills, and most importantly, the attitude to be an exceptionally sharp tip of the spear. But for selfish reasons, I am glad he ended up in Grand Forks. With my particular circumstances as a tanker copilot, I needed to get sharp quickly in the airplane, and I never would have challenged myself in the cockpit the way he challenged me. Yes, we broke some rules. Actually, a couple of times, we broke all the rules and had some memorable adventures doing it. As I look back on it though, and track our inability to consistently follow those rules, if someone had asked, "If you aren't caught, did it really happen?" I think you know what our response would be.

Lastly, and most importantly, I need to acknowledge all the extraordinary help I've been given throughout my life and even prior to it by the Almighty. I have described my half-a-dozen encounters with a guiding voice in my life. But there are also the more subtle, less overt influences that should be discussed. One that struck me as highly improbable but nonetheless true was my mother ending up at the University of Missouri in the mid-1940s.

Women enrolled in college during this time were rare. A poor woman enrolled in college then was even more rare. Most likely the only female in the classroom, the first-born of an elementary school teacher and an angry, underachieving postal clerk, she sat there because of an exceptionally kind married couple. She did herself and her benefactors proud by graduating with honors, but her being there at all has the feel of Divine touch to it.

My father's last-minute change of orders to report to a hospital rather than board the ship heading for England has a similar feeling of the extraordinary. After his release from the hospital, his loss of a kidney made him unfit for combat duty, so he stayed stateside for the remainder of the war. I feel certain there is a story behind his ending up at Mizzou after the war ended. After all, we were talking about my father, and he had plenty of stories to share if he felt like talking. But on this subject, he was silent and Mom, for whatever reason, never mentioned anything about it. Fortunately for me, their paths crossed in Columbia, Missouri, which led to their nuptials in June of 1950.

Fast forward thirty years and I was on my way to play softball at Gifford Park in Omaha with my friend Denny Donahue in the passenger seat of my Camaro. Tom Rossi had already arrived and was discussing our finer attributes with the group of Memorial Day softball players as we were parking the car.

Tom did not include in his list of noteworthy attributes that I never drank alcohol—never had and never would. As a teenager I was unaware of the devastating effects alcohol had on the lives of my parents as they were growing up. Both fathers were alcoholics, and it had ruinous effects on both their families. So, I surprised both myself and my friends by politely refusing when I was offered my first alcoholic beverage as a high school sophomore. I just had a keen sense it would not turn out well if I accepted it, and I needed to keep my wits about me.

Acknowledgments

I subsequently turned that first refusal into a habit. And that habit was about to pay off handsomely. There was an attractive, young woman at the game who initially felt some misgivings about my being invited to play. After Rossi's description of me, I can't say I blame her. But at the party after the game a quart of orange juice I had purchased caught her eye. Her father had serious issues with alcohol, and I was the only one there not drinking besides her. So, orange juice became the starting point of our life together. After Tom's warm-up introduction of me to the group, one would think it would take a miracle for this to happen. Nonetheless, thank you, Tom. At least you didn't mention other things about me that would have sent her fleeing from the field.

At this point I think my guardian angel deserves some well-earned recognition for all its efforts to keep me alive and avoiding scrutiny by the authorities while I was stationed at Grand Forks. I mentioned earlier a large reservoir of good luck always seemed to be available to us when Bob and I decided to do something foolish, and our foolish acts went unreported. I think our "large reservoir" wore angelic wings.

During the twenty-six months I was flying the T-38 there, I accumulated a little over one thousand hours in it and five hundred hours of those were with Aboe. We were quite the team, pressing the regulatory limits then routinely pushing beyond them. Yet I had a mission to complete in the KC-135. If we were ever caught in any of our more foolish acts, I was not going to be able to fulfill it. The laws of chance heavily favored a misstep on our part. Yet, somehow, we managed to avoid a reckoning for any of those foolish acts. I am going to credit my guardian angel for tipping the scales of chance in our favor at all those critical moments and allowing us to continue. I know Aboe and I didn't make it easy.

I would be remiss if I did not acknowledge all the invaluable aid I received from Sister Taryn Stark, RSM, who made this work possible. I began this project using pen and paper. I wrote it originally for an audience of two, and my penmanship was barely up to the challenge for that small group. When I found myself being challenged to expand my audience, I was more than reluctant to comply. I was obstinate. I checked and publishers weren't accepting hand-written manuscripts. This meant my work was going to stay within the family, and I was more than just satisfied to leave it at that. I was relieved. My reticent nature on this subject throughout my life made sharing this story difficult. Since I couldn't even type, two seemed like the right number to satisfy my need to share.

Unfortunately for me, the challenges to my decision to withhold readership not only persisted, but they also increased. I finally had to acknowledge I needed to change my mind about this if I wanted to avoid becoming an insomniac. Yet, the same issues remained with my parchment-and-quill grasp of word-processing technology. I decided if this were going to work, I would need someone of faith who had the technological skills I lacked and was willing to sacrifice the time and effort necessary to finish it with me. It was no small task, and I knew I would be asking a lot from this individual. I didn't know where to begin to search for such a person, so I prayed for guidance while I was alone in the church. And through a remarkable set of coincidences that took place in that sacred structure, I was given my answer. Sister Taryn teaches technology skills to the elementary students across the street from our church, and

Acknowledgments

after reading my hand-written letter pleading for her help, she agreed unconditionally. She was even capable of deciphering my childlike scrawl masquerading as penmanship in the letter I left for her at the school office. That alone should confirm she was God's chosen!

Sister Taryn not only proved selfless but tireless in her efforts to help. She provided a printed copy of my work months ahead of her estimated date of completion that included a grammar check on the project. I was dumbfounded as I reviewed it with her. There was no way I could have done what she did for me. And she did it so unselfishly, devoting many hours of her time because someone she occasionally saw at weekday Mass surprised her with a request. God really knew what he was doing when he sent her my way. That also goes for all the nuns I encountered during my life—even Sister Herman.

Early in this acknowledgment portion of the memoir I mentioned wanting to show a direction and theme. The theme I will leave up to you, but after reading through all these pages I hope you agree the direction is potentially heavenward. I had some extraordinary help in my life, and it began before I was even conceived. My parents had awful early lives, yet they were able to overcome those difficulties and challenges to become wonderful, faithful individuals. My siblings and I were the blessed beneficiaries of this. Despite my shallow to nonexistent belief in God I was given Providential guidance at critical points in my life. And how did I respond? By following the advice while doing my level best to avoid examining its origins. Yet it reached such an obvious level of intercession that even someone as stubborn and strong-willed as me had to finally acknowledge God's hand in all this. As I wrote earlier, this happened at Matthew's birth. In the delivery room, shortly after our son arrived, I was being flooded with the realization this was only possible through God's exceptional grace toward Denise and me when we learned it was a boy. To this wonderful news I responded with, "Great, a son. I have someone to help me with the lawn." It was either Irish sarcasm or weeping for joy at both the birth of our son and rebirth of my faith. I struggled but managed to stay in character and went with the sarcasm. You can better understand now why it took so long for me to come back to my faith. The Irish can be unbelievably hardheaded. Just ask the English.

But the important fact in all this is I did come back. Studying the Bible and other resources along with prayer, the Rosary, and daily Mass made a big difference. I thank God He didn't take me earlier so I could discover this. Now I feel an obligation to pass all this along to you.

Crazy as this sounds, and I understand just how crazy it does sound, it happened as I described. I hope you will believe your seemingly deranged father and allow religious faith to enter your lives. You and your life will change for the better. This is not to say your life will be free of challenges and suffering. Quite the contrary. Expect them. Jesus says in Luke 9:23-24, "If any man would come after Me, let him deny himself and take up his cross daily and follow Me. For whoever would save his life will lose it and whoever loses his life for my sake, he will save it." We all must suffer in life, just as our Savior did. How well we deal with it will help determine our path in salvation. Would you allow me to pass on some simple, yet profound advice given to me by those nuns back at St. John's elementary school in Davison, Michigan?

Acknowledgments

When suffering enters your life—whether it's physical or emotional, minor or devastating, straightforward or confounding—try to "offer it up." Show our Savior you understand and appreciate His coming into our world, undergoing all the same physical and emotional travails involved with being born human, teaching us how we should live our lives and His ultimate sacrifice for our sakes. Tell Him you will follow His example, pick up your cross every day as an act of appreciation for the love He has shown us and offer it as a sacrifice. And by doing so you will be punching your ticket into salvation.

At this point I will make my last pitch for coming back to the Church and its sacraments in case you ignore the favors I requested earlier. There is a famous Frenchman named Blaise Pascal who lived in the seventeenth century. He was quite an accomplished individual known for his works in physics, mathematics, philosophy, and theology. He combined his knowledge in mathematics and theology to come up with the rationalization for a belief in God using probability theory. It became known as Pascal's Wager. Stated simply, the finite pleasures you forego in this life by following Christ's teachings, weighed against the infinite reward achieved in the eternal afterlife are incomparable. In terms of risk and reward, choosing those finite pleasures or even betting with your life that hell, or an afterlife, doesn't exist is therefore a fool's wager. Better to live a life modeled by Jesus, following His commandments, than risk losing heaven and suffering for eternity in hell. Mark, in his gospel, makes a similar appeal when he writes, "What does it profit a man to gain the whole world, yet forfeit his soul?"

So, it's a stark choice facing everyone. Does this life end with the last beat of the heart, with nothing to follow as I thought earlier? Or is it a transit stop on the way to eternity? It's very easy to lose sight of this choice as we go about our day-to-day living, but it can't be ignored indefinitely. The tracks only go in two directions once life has run its course, and I hope this effort of mine helps you make it into the right passenger car. But if you're still uncertain about your choice after everything I have written, my final piece of advice for you is to seek out the train with Mr. Pascal acting as conductor. Allow him to be the one who punches your ticket for the journey. I look forward to greeting you at the end of the line.

www.ingramcontent.com/pod-product-compliance
Lightning Source LLC
LaVergne TN
LVHW051057080426
835508LV00019B/1932